CREATIVE SOC

The Practice of Social Work

General editors: Bill Jordan and Jean Packman

Creative Social Work

Edited by
DAVID BRANDON
BILL JORDAN

Basil Blackwell · Oxford

© Basil Blackwell Publisher 1979

First published 1979 by
Basil Blackwell Publisher Ltd.
5 Alfred Street
Oxford OX1 4HB

British Library Cataloguing in Publication Data

Brandon David
    Creative social work — (The practice of social work series).
    1. Social service - Great Britain - Case studies
    I. Title   II. Jordan, Bill   III. Series
    361.3′0941   HV245

ISBN 0 631 11831 4 Hardback
      0 631 11841 1 Paperback

Reproduced from copy supplied
printed and bound in Great Britain
by Billing and Sons Limited
Guildford, London, Oxford, Worcester

Contents

vi

Introduction

DAVID BRANDON and BILL JORDAN

I know many people, so-called monks, good social workers and so on, who have trained themselves not to be angry. But the real flame has gone, they never had it, they are kind, generous people, they will help you, will give you their money, their coat, their shelter, but the real thing is nowhere there. I want to find out how to let this thing flower in us; once it flowers you can't destroy it.

(Krishnamurti, *Beginnings of Learning,* Penguin, 1978)

"Creative social work" sounds like a paradox. Most people's stereotype of a social worker — to some extent reflected in the literature of the profession — is of a profoundly uncreative being, a passive, reasonable, dull, smiling sponge who soothes troubled surfaces with abundant soft soap; a Uriah Heep figure without the redeeming evil intentions. When new social work students are asked to play the role of a helper, they often produce a performance as narrow and rigid as the most institutionalized client.

Powerful social forces push social workers into restricted roles. There is a strong public expectation that they should be nicely and inoffensively helpful, never angry or disturbing. Some clients paralyse social workers' imagination and creativity with threatening and disruptive demands, but most see them as rather low-ranking officials of whom little is to be expected. Increasingly, social workers are a small part of large local government organizations and required to follow standardized procedures in processing human problems.

1

Occasionally, they are forced to take life or death decisions or to exercise legal powers of compulsion. At these times there are particularly strong pressures from both inside and outside their agencies to take few risks and to cover themselves against complaints.

However, social workers (including ourselves) must accept a great deal of responsibility for self-imposed strait-jacketing. We feel safer (even when resentful) in following the beaten path, avoiding pain and danger and thereby missing opportunities for innovation and adventure. There is ample scope to blame others for our own failure to develop and change. We can blame unresponsive clients, or rigid organizations, or the ignorance of the community for our own complacency and drifting. We can console ourselves that creativity is constantly frustrated by factors beyond our control, preventing us from doing "real" social work and from realizing our full potential.

The essays in this book are descriptions of attempts to break out of these constraints and to be creative. The authors come from a variety of backgrounds and work in very different settings, each with its own particular restrictions and problems. Some, like Philippa Seligman, have found agencies in which they are free to experiment and improvise. For others, like Noel Davies, creativity lies in the challenge of finding ways through or round the rigidities of our most traditional and repressive institutions. Some are simply self-confessed individualists like ourselves; others, like Gwen James and Robin Hall, have built up teams to support each other's initiatives and implement new policies.

It is difficult to generalize about what social work might be, never mind what might make it creative, from these very different contributions. It could well be that the personal skills and qualities for a creative probation officer are different from those required in creative residential work. However, there are certain themes that run through all the chapters and which may provide clues as to the sources of creativity within the authors' personalities and methods.

The first and most obvious quality of a creative social worker is self-confidence — not of the brash variety, but the kind that comes from security of identity, from knowing one's own boundaries and limits as a means of recognizing and respecting others'. The stereotyped uncreative social worker is restricted by a limited range of responses which are associated with being "helpful" but whose effect is paradoxically lifeless, negative and oppressive. With self-confidence, the social worker feels free to use a far wider range of his attributes and emotions than originally seemed "safe". He learns to make a positive use of feelings he previously feared as damaging and destructive, and to rely more on intuition. He allows himself to take part in activities that he might once have considered "unprofessional". His sphere of operations also becomes wider, as he becomes more aware of more factors that can be influences relevant to both his own and the clients' lives. This expansion of professional activity can occur across many dimensions. In Noel Davies' case, it meant more emphasis on larger-scale political activity; for David Smith it meant closer attention to the detail of apparently humble and practical tasks.

Closely linked with this greater trust of self is an increased respect for clients. A freer approach allows the social worker to enjoy his contacts with most clients, to like them better and so share more of himself with them. On the one hand, the social worker becomes less afraid of making a fool of himself; on the other he can enter into more of a partnership with clients, recognizing their strengths and developing them. Instead of being envious of their wildness or fecklessness, he can find opportunities for taking part in activities that take them both far beyond the stereotypes of social worker and client. Martin Seddon's essay on New Careers shows how this notion of sharing can be explored by enabling clients to learn to be social workers. Bill Jordan writes about some of the implications of being part of the same community as the clients over a long period of time. But running through all the chapters, there is this creativeness of sharing, sometimes to the point where there is a kind of fusion between client and social worker.

As a means to this end, the authors illustrate the importance of flexibility in what they are as well as in what they do. They all describe ways in which they respond less predictably to clients' needs. As David Brandon illustrates, even a clever and knowledgeable counsellor can be stiff-necked and ritualistic. One important key is to become a better listener, to be able to 'hear' not only the content but also the colour of what the client is saying. You may then be less ready to rush in with ready answers, interpretations and theoretical analyses. It certainly involves travelling over some new territory, and being open-minded enough to throw away cherished solutions, and even to say that you do not know what the solution might be.

All this may sound as if creative social work means just doing what comes naturally. That is not what we wish to suggest. In these essays we advocate a substantial element of self-discipline. However, much of this consists in overcoming well-established and often Pavlovian responses to situations in which help is required by other people. The resources for giving genuine help are present in all of us; what has to be learnt, usually slowly and painfully, is how to uncover those resources and to share them.

Many situations that social workers encounter are outside the run of ordinary human experience. Forced by the nature of our work to stay close to what is bizarre, alarming or repulsive, we "naturally" become tense, cautious and limited. This sometimes involves closing out the surprising and the overwhelming; becoming frightened and rigid. Only if we experience this fully can we then bring into play aspects of our feelings and imaginations that require security to flourish; even then, only more experience and guidance can show us how best to employ them. Some aspects of the social worker's task — for example those involving compulsory admission — however many times they may occur, cannot but cause discomfort and unease. Yet our own troubled minds can enable us to identify sensitively with the client's feelings of impotence and hostility.

The depth of experience needed to facilitate this creative growth is often hard to obtain. Social services departments spread a vast umbrella over more and more categories of need, and it is easy for professionals simply to shelter under this maternal umbrella without seeing much of the colour of human problems. The sheer volume and breadth of the work prevent social workers from understanding anything or anyone in depth. Gwen James' essay, for example, is an eloquent testimony to the struggle against these kinds of problems.

It is perhaps no coincidence that most of the authors of these essays are specialists of one kind or another. They have found ways of preserving and developing expertise in traditional fields. Many accounts suggest a determined persistence in trying to provide better services for a particular client group, as well as in developing their own skills and knowledge. In some cases, this has meant stepping outside the mainstream of social work organization; in most it has meant choosing an alternative to the conventional career of promotion into managerial posts.

Just as the administration of social work has become "generic", so theories of social work practice have increasingly generalized, attempting to span the whole range of activities undertaken by social workers. We feel that considerable intellectual energy has been wasted in trying to frame general theories of social work — efforts akin to that of Alastair MacIntyre's friend who spent a lifetime framing a general theory of holes, without reference to their different purposes.[1]

These essays should be read as separate contributions to creative work in each of the fields they cover; they offer no general theory of social work, holes or creativity. Collectively, they give indications of what creative social work is *not*. For instance, it is not confined to any particular sort of agency, voluntary or statutory. It is not inconsistent with compulsory powers, residential provision, even with psychiatric hospitalisation or imprisonment. It is not the prerogative of any particular school of thought or practice.

We had difficulty in deciding how to order the various chapters. In the end we opted to begin with Keith Wilding's account of a social work department in Glasgow (Strathclyde), one of the bleakest and most deprived areas in Europe. This essay provides a basis from which other contributions can be read. It is an essay full of confusion and humanity, the essential stuff of which social work is made.

Social work has its roots in the kind of deprivation and demoralization endemic in areas like Glasgow. It must ultimately stand or fall by its contribution in such conditions. That is its heritage. For social workers, as well as for the population at large, life can become largely a matter of survival and endurance, of patching together some meaning and significance as well as much pain and stress. The conditions of work that Keith Wilding describes are reminiscent of George Konrad's novel "The Caseworker". Like Konrad, he is vividly aware of the inadequacy of his "bureaucratic solutions" to the suffering he encounters. His conclusion might well be expressed in the final words of "The Caseworker":

"Let all those come who want to; one of us will talk, the other will listen; at least we shall be together."[2]

REFERENCES

1. A. MacIntyre, 'Is a comparative science of politics possible?' in P. Laslett, W. Runciman and Q. Skinner (Eds.), *Philosophy, Politics and Society* — Fourth Series, Blackwell, 1972.
2. George Konrad, *The Caseworker,* Hutchinson, 1975, p. 172.

1   We, the willing . . . .

KEITH WILDING

It is Friday afternoon, one of those Friday afternoons that become legendary in social work departments, the sort that passes into departmental folklore and recurs in social workers' nightmares.

Four o'clock: two inspectors of the R.S.S.P.C.C. enter with a partially completed place of safety order on a four-year-old child, who for various reasons had been referred some weeks previously. They relate a story of suspected abuse and it is decided that since I know the family I should investigate.

Four-thirty: I stand shivering outside the door of a cheerless block of modern tenement flats in a Glasgow housing scheme. The flat is on the ground floor and a bitingly cold wind blows through the close. It is snowing. I try to tell myself that the snow and the wind are responsible for my shivering. But I am just plain scared of facing the anger and the tears, the inevitable consequences of my visit. I have worked in this part of the world for nearly three years and never have I become used to these damned visits. The anger will be directed against me because I am the visible instrument of the family's misfortune. I can understand it but never get used to it.

Six o'clock: mother, stepfather, child, social worker, social work assistant (social worker's friend and moral supporter) are at the Royal Hospital for Sick Children. Examination, more tears, more anger, and the child, who is extensively bruised, is admitted to the hospital.

Eight o'clock: mother returns home still steadfastly denying that she has touched the child. Her husband has gone off to do night-shift and is not interested in "casework support" anyway. If it comes to that, by eight o'clock, tired, hungry and emotionally spent, none of us are much interested in "casework support". It will all have to wait until the following week. I am going away for the weekend and I am already four hours late. The mother has to face the night and most of the weekend alone.

The following week I have two similar referrals. One keeps me out until midnight; the other is a transfer from another local authority and all is quiet — someone else had done the legwork sometime before.

To the layman this sort of investigation is "the stuff of social work". It has all the elements of excitement and crisis and of "rescue" — the sort that produces television drama and recruitment literature. It does take time and energy and some courage and emotional resource but it can, paradoxically, be described as the "easy" part of social work. It is reasonably easy to justify intervention and there is a fairly clear-cut, short term objective that, in the eyes of the public, is a laudable aim.

The "hard" part is the long haul of support and supervision, walking the tightrope between the needs of the child, of the parents, of the system, and of the social worker. The hard part is finding enough time between the incessant demands to fit in all the things that do not come and take hold of you and *demand* time. The hard part is working in situations where public approval is not readily forthcoming.

Apart from the crises, a social worker can spend hours negotiating the minefield of the 'A' code (Supplementary Benefits), the house letting regulations, or the joint memoranda on fuel debts on behalf of bewildered clients. Often it is not only the clients who are bewildered! A good deal of time is spent in filling in forms — referral forms, Department of Health and Social Security (D.H.S.S.) forms, fuel board forms, forms for one's own files, forms for head-quarters, or writing letters that explain, implore or inform. All of this brings one into contact with varying degrees of distress brought about by conflict — within the family, within the person, with society, and, not infrequently, an amalgam of all three, each exacerbating the other in subtle and not so subtle ways.

The team in Glasgow of which I was a member covered an area where the vast majority lived in local authority housing. My patch was the nicest bit, containing the only slice of owner-occupied territory in the area. There was a high rate of unemployment; higher than the Strathclyde Regional average, which in turn is higher than the national average. The level of service expectation was low and many of our regular customers had a love-hate relationship with "the Welfare" to whom they came with increasing regularity for advice, or representation in their particular conflict. The referral rate was high (between twenty and thirty each day was usual, over thirty was busy) and many problems brought to the department affected the basic concerns of life — food, clothing, heat, light, and liberty — things that most of us take for granted. Similar problems were taken to the Citizens Advice Bureau who shared the load and *reduced* the referral rate to our department from what it had been in *"the good old days"*.

It is hard for many people to accept that in our much vaunted Welfare State there are people living at subsistence level, pressurized by the norms of the rest of us, who feel in some way inferior because of their poverty. I used to wonder what all that social work training was for, since experience in advocacy, and an ability to read small print (quickly, so that many people would not be kept waiting too long) would have been a far more suitable training than philosophical discussions about clients' rights of self-determination. Since most of our clients were reduced to the simple choice of "take it or leave it", any discussion about the merits of self-determination seemed largely academic.

Because there were so many problems associated with poverty, the system developed a series of "bureaucratic solutions" to deal with fuel debts or rent arrears. Applications could be made, theoretically by the client, to the Supplementary Benefits Commission (S.B.C.) for rent and fuel costs to be paid directly to the supplier of the service involved. This worked well with fixed rent payments but the amounts required by the fuel boards, particularly the electricity board, were usually far above the amounts prescribed in S.B.C. regulations. Thus, what was supposed to be a calculated subsistence income was reduced well below the officially recognized subsistence level — which many would argue was set too low anyway — by the fuel bills. Because of the sheer volume of problems, "bureaucratic solutions" were often used and much welcomed by area team social workers. They were frequently instrumental in reducing real individual distress and hardship or, failing that, in containing the state of affairs so that there was no rapid deterioration. Nonetheless, the pressure of poverty affected many people.

Not everyone under pressure beat their children so severely that they bruised them. Looking at the circumstances in which many young mothers found themselves I am surprised that more of them did not batter children. However, there are less obvious ways of "abusing" children and not all of them can be blamed on the parents.

On one occasion, a single mother and her baby appeared in the office when I was on duty. It was obvious from her bedraggled appearance and general air of listlessness that she had come to us with little hope merely because the department was the last in a long line of offices. She had two electricity bills. One was for the flat in which she had just been housed while the other was for the property in which she had been squatting. She had no friends or relatives in our area, no food, no money, a six month old baby, and formal notice about disconnection of the electricity supply. It is easy but somewhat unhelpful to say "it serves her right" or "it's her own fault" and all the other words of wisdom that are often emitted from the mouths of the most educated laymen.

The system's answer, and it must be given credit for trying to find an answer, was fairly straightforward. There are clear guidelines as to what to do about destitution. An application is made to the D.H.S.S. for fuel direct payments. The client's fuel supply is then safeguarded and the fuel board get their money. However, this was one of those cases where large weekly amounts were demanded by the S.S.E.B. and, at the risk of being over-emotional and melodramatic, the arrangement was literally taking food out of the baby's mouth because so much was being spent on fuel. By using unhesitatingly the solution provided by the bureaucratic system in which we all live, was I contributing to the abuse of that child? Is it only when the bruises show that "casework support" is necessary?

The young woman received no further support from me. She had presented a problem that had been "solved". I largely ignored the magnitude of the personal distress behind it. If all similar referrals had been put through for allocation the team would have been swamped. It always left me with the feeling that, in the words of one nineteenth century Christian Socialist, we were far more concerned with helping people in their poverty than helping them out of it. Interviews such as these are not viewed as "the stuff of social work". There is nothing exciting or glamorous about them. They seldom make newspaper headlines. But each social worker has to recognize the existence of the dilemmas produced by this work and seek his own solutions.

Many social workers feel that the only solution offering hope for lasting change is a political one and they shift the focus of their work accordingly. Others, working under day to day pressure, often find it difficult to recognize the existence of wider questions. Many resolve the dilemma by working long and hard and seek out crises to justify to themselves that a worthwhile job is being done.

It is hard to find time to spare for "long-term" work,

especially with the more passive problems. If we compare the couple with the battered child to the girl with the electricity bills, it was far easier to be involved with the former and offer support. There were court and children's panel appearances because of the physical abuse of the child, and in the following months there were several traumatic separations, a couple of housebreakings, an attempted rape, and heartbreak of every kind.

In the case of the girl with the electricity bills the problems were essentially undramatic and focused on the insufficiency of her regular weekly income. The constant daily struggle to survive was just as hard for her as for the family with the child and it may even have been *more* difficult because the authorities were uninterested or unable to alter the root cause of her difficulties.

It can be argued that the system has a counter-productive effect in its attempts to help/control only one type of child abuse. It increases the pressure so much on what must be a fragile set of relationships to begin with that casework support actually contributes to such things as marital breakdown (thereby justifying the need for further casework involvement).

There is no doubt that in some areas of work, notably the physical abuse of children, procedures are designed as much to protect the social worker and the department as to help the child. This is a statement, not a criticism. On several occasions I have been thankful that such procedures exist. The danger is that these procedures and the use of bureaucratic solutions will result in a gradual depersonalizing of the personal social service system.

The hierarchical structure of social work departments is not concerned with the personal dilemmas facing social workers. In cases such as that of our young mother with the electricity bills there are no rules laid down about procedure but long term work is largely a matter of choice on the part of the individual social worker. It then becomes a question of individual priorities and of whose problem takes precedence.

In our department children in care were regarded informally as a "priority", although each social worker operated with his own priorities — implicitly or explicitly. To do so effectively involved planning and organization of time and resources. It required a self-discipline and professionalism that contained little of the layman's image of the Lady Bountiful doing good works.

Criminal behaviour was a major contributor to the workload in our area, and one of the commonest causes of conflict with the system. A good deal of this work should have been "long-term", but (a familiar story) too much time was being spent on interviewing and writing social background reports for courts and for the children's hearings.

Follow up of recommendations was essentially passive and often had to be accorded second place to daily events which claimed time. Probation and supervision became one of those areas of work that you had to choose to become involved with. In my own case I enjoyed writing court reports and I was interested in the probation side of the work. Even so I do not regard myself as having done it very effectively. On occasions I would come across painful situations that would prick my conscience sufficiently to spur me to greater effort.

I interviewed a seventeen-year-old for a report for the High Court on a charge of attempted murder. As the sordid and violent story of the knifing of two youths after a football match emerged, I began to despair for my supervision caseload. This youth was unemployed, inarticulate, scared, and had a history of truancy, children's panel appearances, and court appearances on fairly minor breach of the peace charges. He talked of the drinking, the bravado, the casual violence that lead up to the incident. His story could have come from any one of numerous boys in the area if they had been faced with the same precipitating factors. It made me wonder. If I had allocated more time to him in the past would he be in this position? He was sentenced to eight years imprisonment in a young offenders institution and I tried a little harder with the boys that were left.

Because it was realized that so little time could be allocated to long-term involvement, few recommendations of probation were made to courts. The result was that the probation aspect of the service was contracting. Increasingly, courts only asked for reports where the law required them before a custodial sentence could be imposed. Social workers began to resent writing reports where the outcome was more or less a foregone conclusion. This "Catch Twenty-Two" had an additional twist since it was virtually always the case that a custodial sentence on a young offender resulted in a period of after-care. In practice after-care supervision had been largely abandoned though it remained a statutory responsibility; it increased the paper work, and made everyone realize that here was yet another area of the work unsatisfactorily covered. Because it was essentially passive it could be left at the bottom of everyone's list of priorities so that time could be devoted to more "deserving" cases.

A similar situation existed with supervision orders from the children's panel. Inadequate supervision often led to further offences which meant more time had to be spent writing further reports and attending further hearings. Consequently, less and less time was left for actually supervising children at home or in residential establishments.

In an area where there were large numbers of children referred for offences and/or truancy it was often argued that "patting them on the head" and sending them off to see a social worker, who hadn't the time to see them anyway, was a largely pointless exercise. This is perhaps a caricature of what happened but it was commonly believed to be true. In some instances, putting a child on supervision was pointless. We often felt this with older kids referred for truancy. Social workers argued that this was an area that ought to be pushed back to the schools and education services. The amount of influence that social workers could have at this late stage was minimal. Often the solution to chronic truancy was thought to be a residential placement. Members of the panel would accordingly instruct the social worker to seek a List D school (formerly approved school) place.

These schools had long waiting lists and there was inevitably confusion about whether List D schools were the ultimate punishment for truancy or non-cooperation when on supervision, or whether they were a separate therapeutic tool in their own right. This problem was perhaps more acute in the assessment centres. Bulging at the seams, they were becoming holding units for the more intractable children and had little or no time to spare for assessment. Even if they could give time, there was always the problem that the appropriate resource was unlikely to have a vacancy for some considerable time.

Social workers in area teams, residential workers, enforcement agencies, parents and children, each had their own views on how residential provision in this field should operate. It is hardly surprising, therefore, that residential institutions failed to please everyone. Indeed, some managed singularly to please no-one at all.

With the varying demands made upon them by the system and by the clients, and the need, for various reasons, to side-step, ignore, or resort to second best, it is no wonder that social workers resort — to a greater or lesser extent — to defence mechanisms of their own. By the end of a week battle fatigue is a familiar complaint. It is associated with being under constant bombardment while simultaneously trying to organize forces for an assault on the source of the bombardment — on the causes rather than the manifestations of the problems. It is impossible to achieve any resounding victory for it is not that sort of war. It is a guerilla war involving constant re-appraisal of who your friends are and which weapons will be the most effective in the light of the changing circumstances in which the war is being fought. The problem with a long guerilla war is that it leads to a blunting of the capacity to share and understand the pain that a problem, which you have seen on many occasions, is causing an individual who has never previously experienced it.

There are times when the main enemies are doubt and frustration within oneself. There is frustration with the apparently intractable nature of the problems and doubt that they are solvable. It is frustrating to have to choose priorities knowing that by doing so others are being left in misery because they are judged to be "less important". One has doubts about the unavoidable moral choices thrust upon one. Doubt is engendered by the contradictions of being a local government official, the man from "the Welfare", the representative of the system that expects its rules to be upheld, and the need to represent a client against the very system of which one is an integral part.

On the occasions when providing a service means representing the client against the system itself, the social worker often has to ignore, collude with, or help with fiddles of one sort or another. In these instances choices have to be made. I made mine and have found some of them difficult to live with.

There are some compensations, the occasional glimpse of light at the end of the tunnel. The family of five that is helped through a bad patch with a little harmless fiddling of the system; the old couple who are saved from eviction, thanks to a little fast talking, a little coercion, and the good offices of the Royal Naval Benevolent Association; the child in care, who, after two years in hospital, is placed more appropriately and begins to settle; the lad who, after being in three List D schools and expelled from them all, finally settles for a full eight months in one place, is discharged home and finds a job.

Each social worker can find similar rays of hope from his client contact in Glasgow; each of us was sustained by colleagues when these rays were rare. The team was no band of angels and from time to time we grated on each other, but there was always someone who would listen to a good moan and help preserve one's sanity. I know the battered social worker syndrome has become a cliché but there were occasions when I *felt* battered. Then again, perhaps that's just my defence.

2 An Experience of Residential Life

ROBIN HALL

My residential experience — including working in Scottish borstals — goes back twelve years. Each of my moves has been a result of uneasiness about the relevance of a particular setting to the wider world from which the residents come and to which they one day return. While I was in a borstal that was physically closed off from the outside world and that had its inmates perform strange rituals in the name of discipline and training, I wondered how on earth the residents could put their borstal experience to any use on discharge. I then moved to an approved school, where the length of time a pupil stayed in the school was directly determined by his behaviour in it. The message was clear: an approved school must be a bad place to be in since you have been sent here by a court for having committed offences, but if you behave yourself and play the system intelligently, we'll get you out of here quickly.

In 1971, I was appointed Head of Thornly Park School in Paisley, which is a few miles south-west of Glasgow, and in the middle of the most densely populated region in Scotland. My appointment coincided with the implementation of the Social Work (Scotland) Act of 1968. The most challenging aspect of the act related to the handling of children in trouble. It abolished juvenile courts except for certain categories of offences, and, by implication, it abolished approved schools. Instead it created children's hearings before lay people, and instructed local authorities to provide residential

17

establishments to look after those children whom the hearings deemed in need of care away from home. The act was an example of how legislation sometimes anticipates public opinion rather than follows it. It gave rise to doubt and hostility for some of its measures, the commonest being that the new sloppy handling of delinquents would release waves of criminality which would flood the structure of our treasured society.

Nevertheless, there were sufficient people in the community and in social work who were ready to meet the changes in policy. I wanted to use the opportunity of my appointment to test the insights of the act as they related to residential work. As an administrative convenience, approved schools were renamed List D schools until a more apt name could be found for them. This got over the hurdle of the abolition of approved schools, but did not change their ethos with such ease. The schools have had to change from being a punitive resource for the juvenile courts to a residential resource, focusing on the needs of children referred from the hearings because their needs were not being met in the child's family or his immediate surroundings. In our experience the change has been complex, most painful and rewarding. In retrospect, the naïvety of the way in which we pursued change and expected things to come right still brings a smile, but had it not been for that naïve optimism we would never have launched on our course. We had no real foreknowledge of how things would turn out.

Thornly Park was a highly disciplined, obsessionally clean school, permeated with that type of religiosity which could justify the recitation of prayers of self-degradation four times a day, and the highest rate of corporal punishment in the country. On the first day I walked into the school, I made three decisions: to abolish corporal punishment, to replace the morning daily service with a community meeting, and to have a weekly staff meeting. The first measure, I thought, would be received as a declaration of good will and willingness to tackle the whole area of authority in a new and shared way. The other two measures would introduce processes of communication and debate allowing the speed of change to be dictated by those people most likely to be affected.

First reactions to these changes were numbed shock, disbelief, and fear. The boy who volunteered to be secretary to the community meeting absconded on the following day when he realized he was expected to read out the minutes of the previous meeting. Staff clung to the belief that the only effective way of insuring against anarchy was the belt for the kids and clear directives for the staff. One example of such a directive was: "If you are on duty in the yard during the boys' break time, stand by the gateway (the only means of escape) and make sure no-one goes through. Don't be fooled into leaving your post to sort out a fight which is going on at the far corner of the yard. It will be sure to be a decoy to lure you away and enable others to abscond."

These first reactions were followed either by a blind belief that the headmaster knew what he was doing and that all would come out for the best, or by an assertion that the headmaster was mad and that the school would blow up within a fortnight. Both reactions produced the same effect: staff felt unable to handle events as they arose or claimed they had no responsibility for the insane organization. A member of staff on duty was observed standing at the door of a recreation room where boys were jumping up and down on a piano. When asked why he was not doing anything about restraining them, his reply was that that was the new policy: anything went.

Community meetings were odd affairs. We all sat in three concentric circles, composed of about eighty children and thirty staff. We knew that we could not begin to work with people's personal problems in a meeting that size, but it was at least a forum where the necessary rules of living together could be worked out and breaches of those rules discussed. However, we had underestimated the strength of the no grassing code. This code states quite simply that nothing which happens in the underlife of an institution ever gets passed on to the staff group. The boys, aged thirteen to sixteen, had already been indoctrinated by their previous experience of adults into adopting the prisoner mentality as their only means of survival. We had also underestimated the degree of suspicion and distrust of adults, which had already become hardened. If adults lorded it about with a strap under their jackets, they at least conformed to the kids' image of them and could be handled according to the kids' accumulated experience of such people. But if adults said such crazy things as "Let's set up meetings together so that we can discuss the various difficulties as they arise", the children were confused because of the absence of any experience in their lives of this way of confronting problems.

The first few months were dominated, therefore, by disbelief, silence, and revolt. We were naïve to think that children were going to welcome liberating statements from the same adults who had, a few months earlier, been behaving in a quite different manner. The situation was not helped by those adults who did not believe in their own liberating statements themselves, but transparently paid lip service to them. The boys came to the conclusion that they had inherited a madman for a headmaster and proceeded to prove it. They nearly succeeded.

Suddenly — it may have had something to do with Christmas — the boys were heard to refer to the school as "this new system which we are trying to work". The following months were almost idyllic. Staff and pupils felt they almost had something new within their grasp, and seemed determined to make sense of it. Initiative for change did indeed come from the community and staff meetings. For example, the most effective way of keeping the large number of inmates in the institution clean had been to have a shower parade, followed by a detailed inspection of naked bodies. Until this time the indignity of such a procedure had not crossed the minds of staff or pupils. One day, in the community meeting, a boy accused a member of staff of being a "poof" because of his apparent enthusiasm for inspecting naked boys. It looked as though the roof might fall in. Instead, the shattering realization of the enormity of that practice which had gone on unhindered for fifty years led us to the simple suggestion that such institutionalized ways of handling children be abandoned and that we should start to introduce a more personalized form of care.

Far from changing too quickly, we could not change fast enough. The process had a momentum of its own and for many years we were simply running to catch up. The inevitable result of abandoning mass washings and concentrating on helping children to take a personal interest and responsibility in the way they looked after themselves, was that the boys became dirtier and smellier. Nevertheless, things were catching on. The morning community meeting found itself discussing bullying and went silent. Because nothing was resolved, a crisis meeting as called after tea, and again the same silence hung over the meeting. Suddenly, a little pocket-sized boy walked around the large assembly and slowly picked out the bullies. The drama of that night was not only that the bullies made grudging noises about controlling their habits, but also that the little boy's protest did not bring down the wrath of the others upon him. Not a hair of his head was harmed. The first hint of the possibility of staff and pupils achieving some common ground had been made.

The honeymoon was short lived. The boys who had become excited about taking an active part in creating a new system left before the system had taken root. Newcomers, still believing that they had been sent for punishment, couldn't believe their luck in finding themselves in a "permissive" setting. The difference between responsible choice and being slaves of whim was not then clear to them and at that time the staff were not sufficiently confident of the boy's ability to deal with such subtleties. The next two-and-a-half years were marked by a see-saw of fortunes. There were periods of suspicion and devil-may-care attitudes when absconding abounded, vandalism in the building soared, and the number of offences committed outside the school rose alarmingly. Doubts within the staff about the damage done to the boys far outweighed their brave little statements that the boys were learning a lot about themselves. Then there would be periods of growth when the children began to make use of their time, began to trust staff with their own fears, allowed work to be done with their families, and began to understand something of the dynamics of a large group trying to evolve a system of living and working together.

Disaster struck during one of the "down swings". We had a number of fire-raisers in the school and one in particular took great pleasure in starting little fires, and waiting until they had caught hold. He would then rush to raise the alarm, and wait excitedly for the fire engines to arrive. On one of these occasions the fire took more quickly than expected, licked its way into the roof, and brought down the whole building. A fire which started at lunchtime in March, 1975, left us without a school by the middle of the afternoon, and faced with the problem of what to do with the seventy frightened boys. At Thornly Park we talk of "the Fire" as most people talk of "the Flood". The event heralded a fresh relationship between pupils and staff.

Since our classrooms had not been affected we held onto a nucleus of twenty boys who came to us as day pupils while we hastily put up temporary residential accommodation. By the end of August, we were able to offer a residential resource, and invited our nucleus to apply. Fifteen did so, since things were strained at home; two had reached leaving age anyway, and three opted to stay on as day pupils because they had found home life tolerable once again. The first few months were riddled with tension. Staff had barely recovered from the fire and needed not only to be nurtured but reminded of their skills in order to regain their confidence. Pupils were trying to find a way of saying that they did not want to return to the days when adults and children vied with each other for a monopoly on authority.

We had a group of adults and children who had been

scarred by a frightening event but who had, through the event, discovered that they wanted to be together. Attitudes about being a bad boy and getting sent away, and approved school being places for punishment, still prevailed in the outside world. There was a mixture of feeling both good and bad about being at Thornly. The best that boys and staff could do was to make agreements that it was really not on to light fires in the buildings and go on midnight forays in the neighbourhood. People were being over friendly with each other out of sheer nervousness and the first clash was sure to come.

Predictably, it arose over the question of fire. There had been a long standing rule that although boys were allowed to smoke they were not allowed to carry matches for fear of irresponsible use. The rule still stood, and when we first discovered that it had been broken in our beloved wooden huts that had now become our school, there was a panic which I feel ashamed to recall. Mercifully, the boys seemed less worried than we did. Through simple but skilful negotiation in the community meetings, they persuaded the staff that another fire could be more effectively prevented by allowing boys to carry matches and involving them in responsibility for some control over those using matches stupidly than by assuming that all boys with matches were potential fire-mongers.

The intervening years have seen a growing openness in the relationship between pupils and staff and, just as significantly, among the boys themselves. First names crept in unobtrusively and were soon widespread. We began to understand more deeply dimensions of warmth and anger, dependence and separateness, choice and discipline, authority and trust, and with these notions in mind I now want to describe the present day.

Emphasis is placed on the pre-admission interview. Before a boy is received into the school, he visits us with his family and field social worker. This usually takes place shortly after the children's hearing has decided to place the child on a residential supervision order. The mood of the parents is usually one of either anger or guilt. Unless the hearing has been very skilful, the parents will feel judged unfit to look after their son, and will rarely be eager to meet those people — ourselves — singled out as able to do the job better. If this barrier is not melted, any continued relationship will be fraught with misunderstanding. We go to great lengths to help parents to see that we are not superseding either their role and or their authority. In practice this is not difficult since, unless they want to be rid of him, parents are usually pleased to be assured of continued involvement with their child. The next hurdle is persuading the child that, despite his preconceptions, he is not coming to be punished or "trained" — he may often have come to understand this word as a euphemism for punishment.

It has always been a source of pleasure to watch a newcomer and his parents relax before one's eyes, especially after being taken around and entertained to tea by a couple of boys in the school. It may be a case of Hobson's choice since the child already knows that he has to go somewhere, but he does at this stage have the responsibility of choosing whether to come to Thornley Park or opt for some other place. Sadly, but perhaps inevitably, the relief and euphoria of the pre-admission interview which is fanned by the enthusiastic reception from the established pupils wears off shortly after his admission. The place does not turn out to be quite so friendly and carefree as it first appeared. A boy realizes that the difficulties within himself or in his relationships which were instrumental in bringing him here are still with him. Certainly he is relieved for the time being of living in the middle of marital anarchy or on the receiving end of autocratic adult bullies in his day school, but he soon realizes that he is in a setting whose permissiveness challenges his old defences — in self-searching you may find unpleasant things.

The community becomes the focal point in the life of the child and is given enormous importance. Emotions range from boredom, frustration, pain, anger and tears of rage, to contemplation, consensus, resolution and triumph. Boredom and frustration are often linked with the constant incidents of stealing among the boys. "What's the point of bringing up that someone has stolen my shoes? Nothing ever gets done about it." The link between the pain of being stolen from and the indifference of the thief himself is often a painful, hard lesson. Anger often emerges from a confused view of authority. By virtue of previous experience, children are led to believe that they have no authority. All authority is invested in adults and the only way in which a child can express himself is by opposing adults.

There was a boy who was constantly bullied first by his parents, then by most adults around him and finally by boys around him. He learnt how to be subservient to that kind of authority, all the while biding his time. He even learnt how to use accepted authority by making whining complaints about how his fellows treated him. He was always lonely despite his gauche attempts to make friends or curry favour with people who, in his perception, mattered — adults. He wanted to persuade them that not only had he forgiven his parents for horrible acts of violence and neglect and their eventual abandonment, but also that he was desperate to please adults. Our attempts to persuade him that authority came from within, that he was denying his own authority, that he would do well to start from his own sense of value, had a dramatic effect. Having lived for years as a plucked chicken, he changed into a muscular and arrogant cockerel, strutting about his territory seeking out challenges. This was possibly the most painful time of his life. He taunted the women around him for their weakness and inability to care for him, for all women became his mother. He challenged the men around him. He proved that they could not control him unless they were violent and bullies, for all men became his father. His agony was that people around him were prepared to admit to being hurt or challenged and even frightened, and this terrified him. He had not expected to win this battle so easily. He had not expected to discover that authority had nothing to do with one person lording it over another, but rather with attributing value to oneself and, by the same token, enjoying others attributing value to themselves. This boy has a struggle ahead of him since it will be years before he abandons his "dog eat dog" philosophy. He will not forget, however, his experience of people who would not fit into his warped scheme of things.

At the school the resolution of problems is characterized by examples of adults and children bringing sensitive subjects to community meetings, or any meeting which they set up for themselves, and being surprised by the level of trust which actually exists. The question of bullying is the most obvious example. The little boy I previously described had unwittingly fought the battles of many of his successors, among staff as well as pupils. A newcomer who is having a rough time will find himself championed by an established pupil and will have little difficulty in extracting an agreement to give him more space. This may not guarantee him peace throughout his stay in the school but it will encourage him to believe that he will be able to raise the matter for himself the next time. Similarly, the community rarely fails to be moved by a statement from a member of staff that he or she is having difficulty working efficiently because of pressure from either boys or staff.

Each boy has a tutor with whom he discusses his educational timetable. He is given freedom of choice so long as it accords with availability of spaces in subjects and includes some English and Maths. Because the school and classes are so small, an atmosphere of intimacy pervades it. This is not merely a matter of boys and staff being on first name terms; the two groups experience each other in a way that cuts through professional boundaries. I have never met an unwilling learner since all children are desperate to learn about adulthood. The efforts of teachers not to engage with their pupils on the fascinations of adulthood leave the children no less determined to find out what all the secrets are about. Intimacy in teaching demands a degree of personal knowledge and authority which can handle a hero-worship dependence without being seduced by it on the one hand, and an enraged rejection because the challenge of learning and growth has become too frightening on the other. Under these circumstances, formal teaching relationships cease to have meaning. It becomes as pointless to drag a child to the headmaster for swearing at you, as for wanting to carry your bag.

This relationship is often painful. Our struggle is to steer through the jungle of unnecessary pain to locate zones of potential growth. We meet children who have been dragged through marital anarchy leaving them with jaundiced views of adults and their relationships; who have experienced the bizarre expressions of authority from teachers still working out their own sufferings at the hands of their superiors; or who bear the brunt of panic-stricken members of the public looking for a scapegoat. In terms of individual growth infliction of such pain on children is scandalous. Growing pain is to do with the process of coming together and departing, of selection and rejection, of being real to others. This process is an inexorable part of teaching.

Teaching bursts the boundaries of the classroom, and has links with care. We are dismayed by the assumptions so often made in residential establishments, that care and education are separate functions and should be kept that way. Parenting and the meeting of children's needs is as much the function of the educator as the houseparent. To the child it is the function of those people most significant to him; he is not interested in the niceties of professional differentiation. He notices that one person tends to be the woodwork instructor, and to another he should complain about leaking shoes, but when it comes to facing and making sense of his own destiny, he chooses those who are important to him. Our constant preoccupation is with the boy who chooses no-one.

Teaching is inseparable from encouraging children to exercise choice and to take responsibility for that choice. Its central theme has become the teaching of the difference between choice and whim, and one can only do this in a permissive milieu where choice itself is genuine. Whether it is differentiated from whim depends on whether the people teaching have the skill to be as clear about the nature of responsibility as they are about the nature of choice. This applies to the child who is struggling to decide on the importance of being literate as it does to the child who is faced with the slog that passing exams will entail.

It also applies to the child who is faced with making his mind up about his own life. A boy came to us as very angry and suspicious. What was not at first perceived was his own fear. His father has walked out when he was eight. His mother had become extremely neurotic. He had been expelled from school for repeated truancy and refusing to accept corporal punishment. He had convinced his mother that he was completely out of her control, and he scared us at the pre-admission interview. It was not long, however, before we discovered how frightened he was and then he begged to go home.

In the meantime his mother had remarried which was an invaluable source of support to her, but an added threat to her son who, even at fourteen, had decided he was the master of the house. His struggle was whether to abandon home altogether or to bow to a dominant step-father. He decided to do neither. He faced them both, and himself, and by doing so grew more quickly than he bargained for. From being a recalcitrant child he became a pained and pensive adolescent with not enough sense of security. At least he has broken the theme of competitiveness with his stepfather, but his anger has turned in on itself and he describes his depression as less to do with people around him than with his own destiny. He has come face-to-face with choice as he has never experienced it, and if social work in the school is to mean anything it has to do with staying with him in his dilemma, and waiting for a resolution, rather than manufacturing one.

I also must confront *my* dilemmas — like anger. I can be

forgiven by the boys for being really rather than professionally angry. Children demand a similar forgiveness from me for their anger. I find it hard, sometimes, to maintain balance when a child is screaming abuse one minute and cuddles me the next, but I don't find such displays of feeling incomprehensible. I have come to learn from the children themselves that trust means knowing that your violent feelings are not as destructive as you once feared. The more difficult challenge is to learn how to express and receive loving feelings without being swallowed up.

3   Zen Practice in Social Work

DAVID BRANDON

Sometimes
the noise inside
halts momentarily,
the heart is still
And I can hear you.

Our social work practice is essentially about the communication of genuine warmth and caring; it concerns who we are rather than what we may know. We can recognize that in many social situations either nothing or very little can, or indeed ought, to be done.

Part of this practice lies in perceiving the client not simply as a social victim but as a colleague who is the real expert in his situation. He feels his wants or needs and has developed a system of ordinarily effective survival strategies. Social work is then a process of attempting to widen and illuminate his choices and their costs, to extend autonomy rather than to restrict it. That means watching people fall as well as leap. We are then engaged in enabling people, including ourselves, to seek their own sources of wisdom. Bodidharma, bringer of Zen to China, is reputed to have said — "All know the Way but few travel it."

Our task is to listen to people's expressed wants and to communicate clearly and concretely. There can be few guidelines for such communication, no formulae for the way we talk or what we say. It is important that we be wise rather than clever; that our words and actions should come from the heart rather than from the intellect. We can accept little responsibility for those who never undertake the journey *to knowledge of the 'self'?* although the knowledge that we ourselves are also pilgrims will often be sufficient communication in the beginning.

In one of the sutras, the Buddha is questioned by a Brahmin — "How is it that even though you point the way, so few people enter Nirvana?" He replied, "I will answer if you first reply to another question — which is the way to the nearest village?" The Brahmin responded with clear directions. The Buddha responded, "And what if someone loses their way or never sets out on the journey?" The Brahmin said, "For that I cannot accept responsibility. I gave directions as accurately as possible." The Buddha said, "And so do I."

I am a long way from that kind of detachment. I was visiting one family who were continuously in financial trouble. They lived rather precariously on Supplementary Benefit but understandably enough were ran out of money long before giro day. Their rent arrears were over £150 so the Local Authority housing department was considering eviction. The family and I worked industriously at their financial situation. Even with full S.B.C. entitlement, they just did not have enough money to survive.

I suggested both to the Housing Manager and to the family that the rent be deducted weekly. Both rejected the suggestion. The Manager talked of restricting individual freedoms even though eviction would presumably restrict them more drastically; the family were afraid of even greater financial problems. My advice might not have been good but shortly afterwards the family were transferred to a nearby housing estate. Their new accommodation had one bedroom less and was in an area specially reserved for "bad rent payers."

In Buddhist philosophy, suffering is the gap between expectation and experience. Inside the head there is a technicolour film which contrasts sadly with the black and white world outside. Instead of <u>accepting</u> the outside world, I am continually pained by the way in which events fail to meet my internal expectations. Why don't things and people do what I have scripted them to do? Why am I constantly let down?

A case of granny bashing was referred to our social services office. An elderly, mentally confused woman lived with her only unmarried son. She attended a day centre regularly where she was aggressive and difficult. Her case file was inches thick and dotted with the handwriting of more than a dozen different social workers. All made notes about the mysterious bruises and injuries she sustained over the years.

On my first visit the old lady was at the day centre, so the son and I had the house to ourselves. He was a thin, angular, depressed person. We talked haltingly about everything until we came to crown green bowls. There was a polished silver cup on the mantle, won some years previously. We discovered a common affection for the game — there are some fine bowls gathering dust in my garage.

On my second visit, we also had the house to ourselves. Bruises had been noticed on the old lady's legs, and had conscientiously been noted down by the day centre staff. I asked the son whether his mother was difficult to care for. He began to cry, and blurted out a story about disturbed nights and meals thrown on the floor. I asked him whether he had ever hit her. Through tears, he admitted he had.

Words came in torrents. She had been so difficult over the years, nothing he did was ever good enough, and she accused him of being a homosexual because he had never married — her wrinkled fingers prodded at wounds that only a mother would know about. All those years, he had wanted to tell someone about his way of retaliating — the violence, the nips, punches and kicks. But no-one had asked. Social workers and doctors came and went but seemed afraid to mention it, afraid to know the extent of his violence and desperation.

Just before Christmas, his mother went into a home. To

me, she seemed well cared for by a conscientious staff. To her son, she was shamefully neglected. Every morning brought fresh complaints from him about the meals she had been given, lack of attention to medication, wrong clothing which did not match or suit the weather, hair not properly styled. Early in the New Year, he arrived at the office, determined to take his mother home.

I was angry that all these arrangements had been made and that now he wanted to undo everything. We blustered at one another in the office waiting room. Because Granny was so confused, it was extremely difficult to learn her views, if she had any. Checking with the old people's home, we agreed to let her return but decided to continue supervising both of them by regular visiting at home and watching developments at the day centre.

The son had no transport so he asked me to pick up his mother from the old people's home. I was in a cold chess playing mood, stinking of cleverness. "Although I will do nothing to prevent you from taking your mother home, I do not approve. I will therefore do nothing to assist you." This was neat. But in my heart I wanted to reach out and help a warm homecoming and the start of what, I hoped, would be a better year for them both.

In social work, we are often tempted to draw boundaries around ourselves in a rigid and protective way, a way that smells of fear. Accepting people and the world as they are (especially ourselves) is to begin to melt the ego so that our relations with others can be more diffuse. By doing this we painfully and joyfully learn the language of the heart.

Such a journey means accepting the cobweb part of self, so often hidden from our clients in the "good" work we do. We have to accept the dusty locked rooms of the mind, as well as the "pagodas". Learning that it is "I" who decides, rather arbitrarily anyway, what is pleasant and unpleasant, what is important and what is unimportant. Fully realizing the extent to which I also fall short of the personal expectations of others. Who is the judge and who is the judged?

For me social work is essentially a pilgrimage. It is a journey concerned with helping myself rather than others, a way of more fully knowing myself. It is frequently and necessarily painful because I have so many internal mirages and fantasies. It is a process of unlearning, rather than about acquiring knowledge. So many ideas, concepts, theories and methods are stripped away when one looks directly at those who are suffering. Their personal situations always seem much more complex and changeable than my theories allow.

A theoretical knowledge of social work helps little when handling the daily stress which its practice brings. What is done for clients is usually little and too late. I frequently do not know enough or am insufficiently skillful. How can we improve the way both we and the clients handle stress? Can we permit those potent and optimistic feelings to emerge which form a climate for creative change? Feelings of stress often indicate areas of great structural social inequality but the resulting duodenal ulcers do nothing to further a revolution in anything except surgery. Long term stress may actually impede the growth of potency.

Meditation helps me. I become physically centred in an interview; I focus on the sound of the words spoken by the client so that my personal internal noises are moderated and can hear. I try to respond both to the questioner and the question in an unhurried way, picking out the colour and the content of the communication.

Some time ago, I videotaped an interview with a client. The interview was an uncomfortable experience. I felt that the client was very angry, almost bullying and curt in response to my questions. When I played back the recording my own fear was much more obvious than his aggression.

The following poem sums up the Zen tradition:

> "A special transmission outside the teachings;
> Not standing on written words or letters.
> Direct pointing to the human heart,
> Seeing into its nature and becoming Buddha."

This process may lead us to those personal areas which are frighteningly destructive and despairing. In that place, we stand where many clients have stood; <u>knowing how each other feels in the same place</u> can lead to increased respect for one another.   *empathy*

Social work influenced by Zen cannot be restricted by a set of beliefs or attitudes. It can be a way of actually walking the mountains, a method of training, the basis of which is a <u>gradual opening out into love.</u> Zen is a spiritual blowlamp: an uncovering of the heart through an emptying of the mind.

4　Probation Officers in Prison

DAVID SMITH

Many readers may see little that is creative in prison social work. I agree there is an apparent contradiction here. I sympathize with those in the prison and probation services who argue that probation officers should not work in prisons. But while their arguments reach the same conclusion, they rest on very different assumptions about the nature of prison and the place of social work within it.

I want to examine these arguments in the light of my two years' experience as a probation officer in a long-term maximum security prison. Although I sometimes pretended to have been coerced or cajoled into working in prison, I did actually want to go. Like many probation officers, I had a negative view of prisons. They seemed the most repressive and malignant of all total institutions, and a real threat to the lives of many people — clients and their families. I was interested in the literature about prison, especially in imaginative accounts of prison experiences, and in the year before I went to work inside had prepared myself by being involved in a prison social studies class. This class gave a few men a chance to talk in a reasonably safe, relaxed setting about their experience of prison, of the law, and of loss and failure. It both intrigued and frightened me. Fear was a major motive in going to work in prison. The time had come to face up to the place that expressed most clearly all that I disliked about institutions and what they do to their inmates.

I had some preconceptions about the work. First, that I

36

would try to be a critic of the prison, standing somewhat apart and remaining free to comment on and interpret the institutional action. Related to this was a sense of what "institutionalization" might mean: a drastic restricting of horizons, a lost sense of proportion, and a reduced concern with the world outside. I thought that social work in prison should aim to help prisoners resist these processes, and should thus be intimately connected with after-care. There is an influential idea that all probation officers do in prison is help the authorities to maintain order by means of various sops and palliatives to reduce prisoners' anger and anxiety. I wanted to keep re-asserting the reality of the outside world and its problems, but did not appreciate how strong the tension could become between trying to get prisoners to engage realistically with planning for release and simply helping them to get through their time. Finally, I suspected that prison work would be less professional, less truly social work, and more mundane and mechanical. I imagined, wrongly, that I might keep something more like conventional office hours.

The fundamental question remains: should probation officers be working in prison at all? It has been a perennial question since probation officers were first seconded to prison welfare departments in 1966. I am slightly uneasy about joining in what has become an almost religious debate, but the issue remains important. I believe that the role of both prison officers and prison-based probation officers has traditionally been conceived in an unduly limited, cautious way, and one which considerably restricts creative potential.

Until the end of 1976, probation officers seconded to prisons were officially called prison welfare officers. The name has changed, but it is doubtful if there has been any comparable change in established attitudes. Even probation officers who have worked in prison tend to justify their role in a modest, apologetic way. They are liable to say that while most of it is awful one can get a better attendance at groups when one has a captive audience.[1] The role is awful because it is made up of a range of routine, low-level tasks which are supposed to require no special professional skills — telephoning loved ones, bullying outside probation officers, churning out reports, making token appearances on various prison boards. Dismissive references to "the Welfare" sum up the negative view, deep in the traditions of the prison service, of what social work in prison is or can be. It affects those actually doing the social work as well as the sceptics watching them. The predecessors of probation officers in prison welfare departments (who were employed by the National Association of Discharged Prisoners' Aid Societies) often had a conception of their role that virtually confined them to giving material aid.[2] About 1965 I remember hearing a story of a welfare officer in a prison on the south coast who called at the local probation office asking if he could do voluntary work with them as he did not have enough to do in the prison. He was the only welfare officer for about 300 men.

In recent years the main preoccupation of the Prison Officers' Association (P.O.A.) has been with the apparent loss of status of the main grade prison officer. He is said to have been reduced to a mere turnkey by a long procession of so-called experts who have come into prisons and taken away all the most rewarding aspects of his job.[3] Probation officers are the latest in this demoralizing line. When, in 1963, the Advisory Committee on the Treatment of Offenders was considering who should staff prison welfare departments, the P.O.A. had definite views. Welfare officers should be prison officers, who had "obvious, almost overwhelming advantages to offer";[4] if a system of four grades were introduced, it would improve their career prospects and enable them to carry out all the necessary helping functions in prison. First, there should be "group work" officers, of whom "no great academic learning is necessary"[5], but who would have had some training. Then "rehabilitation officers", who would be trained "to a higher standard". Welfare officers would come third and would be "expert at the intricacies of hire-purchase, National Assistance, pension problems, housing problems, etc." The fourth and highest grade consisted of officers who would work in liaison with the after-care associates.

It is easy to mock this conception of social work in prison, but the prison officers did have some grounds in the current practice of welfare officers for supposing that this was what it was all about. Their ideas were echoed faintly and in a modified form over ten years later, in the Home Office's discussion document on "Social Work in the Custodial Part of the Penal System". This paper concentrates on the idea in the P.O.A.'s memorandum of 1963 which was always most likely to appeal to the probation service: that prison officers should take over the most boring and banal parts of the job — the "welfare" component — and thus free probation officers to get on with the therapy. It suggests that probation officers should stop seeing prisoners as a matter of course and become consultants. Probation officers soon realized the catch: consultants may never get consulted. Nevertheless, the National Association of Probation Officers' working party on social work in prisons recommended that "pilot projects" be set up "associating probation officers and prison officers towards the development of a welfare role for the latter and a new social work role for the former."[6] Experiments along these lines have since gone ahead in a few prisons, without making prison officers noticeably more content. In effect, the proposal invites probation officers to enhance the mystique of casework professionalism by letting prison officers do the tangible, obvious things. The idea that this division of labour will let the therapeutic experts get on with the real work is misconceived. It is part of social work common sense, and an idea accepted by classical casework theory, that "starting where the client is" may mean giving him something by responding in a practical way to the immediate problem he brings — and that this may be a preprequisite for any attempt to use the relationship to help with emotional or interpersonal difficulties.

This, of course, is seen as a huge difficulty. Probation officers are said to be so busy responding to immediate problems, associated primarily with imprisonment, that they have no time for anything else. It has been suggested that they become trapped in a "welfare cycle".[7] In short-term prisons at least prisoners go to probation officers as their link with the outside world. On the whole the officers comply with their requests, the prisoners go away satisfied, and the popular conception of an exclusively "welfare" function is reinforced. It seems odd that probation radicals should blame their colleagues in prisons for doing what they say all social workers should do — respond effectively to the presenting problem and nothing else. Social work in prison is free of the authoritarian constraints that are supposed to vitiate a therapeutic conception of social work in statutory agencies. All contact with a probation officer in prison is voluntary, with the possible exception of parole interviews. It is mostly short-term, task-centred work — if only because an officer with a caseload of 120 can hardly manage anything else.

There is no inherent reason why probation officers in prison should have three times as many cases as their colleagues outside. Giving prisoners supervised access to a telephone would not necessarily undermine prison security. I used sometimes to allow prisoners to speak directly on the telephone rather than make them participate in the conversation at second hand. When doing this, I had to take elaborate precautions to ensure that we were not interrupted. Prison security officers are worried about coded messages being transmitted by telephone — instructions might be given about escape plans, or the organization of rackets back at home. Probation officers, who have exclusive rights over this kind of communication, are generally quite innocent enough to pass on coded messages in all good faith. I was assured that I had lent an unwitting hand in some esoteric piece of criminality when I passed on a message to a man's wife to buy a racing pigeon for an improbably large sum.

My experience was in a relatively uncrowded long-term

prison where, for most of the time, I had a caseload of about sixty-five. I could hardly claim, therefore, to be beset by small but pressing problems which demanded practical action. But I had my share of these. I rarely felt that I was wasting my time in the long afternoons of frantic, frustrating telephone calls to wives, neighbours, solicitors, social workers and debt collectors about the health of children, the missing letters, the lost passports, the sentence of the juvenile court and the impossible hire-purchase payments. I felt silly wandering around Evesham looking for a lubricant to enable a prisoner's pet bird to lay an egg. But with many prisoners, it seemed that my commitment to such drudgery had to be proved before they would trust me with their inner vulnerability and pain. If I had despatched someone else to scour Evesham's pet shops, I do not know how I could have begun. The prison reinforced my suspicion that the brisk professionalism of much writing about short-term work drastically oversimplifies the nature of the helping process.

There are factors at work in prisons that make prison social work difficult — factors more fundamental than the problems that come from high caseloads or the obsession with security. It is true that because different people expect different things of them, probation officers in prisons can experience serious "role strain".[8] For instance, of the twenty-one functions listed in a Home Office circular of 1967 for the guidance of newly-seconded probation officers, nine had to do with prison management rather than with helping individual prisoners. The problem is that by involving themselves in the business of institutional control in this way, probation officers become, in the eyes of prisoners, "rather impotent acolytes" of a despised system, who are therefore useless as social workers. This is an important warning, but one which, on the whole, probation officers seem to have heeded. There is research evidence that probation officers in prison are held in higher esteem by their clients than colleagues outside; some prisoners would not have asked for help if they knew that "the welfare" was a disguised probation

officer.[9] I was alarmed nevertheless by how eager some colleagues were to accept invitations to sit on prison boards and
offer privy counsel to the governor and his assistants. The
problem is that invitations are offered, and taken up, because
they indicate that probation officers are being recognized at
their true worth, respected and accepted as part of a management team. So probation officers sometimes say complacent-
ly that they are helping to maintain control and security, and
justify themselves in professional jargon.

What is control however? Does it not depend on how
people feel, as much as on locks, bolts and bars, and are not
probation officers pre-eminently experts in feelings? An
officer who accepts his part as a manager of the "human
relations" school has switched his allegiance from social
work to the prison, needlessly. Probation officers in their
dealings with courts have to balance similar contradictions.
To work in the interests of clients they have to keep open
lines of communication with the court and retain some credibility in the eyes of sentencers, but this does not usually mean
that they identify themselves with the court and its objectives.
The problem in prison is more difficult, because the pressure
of the different sets of expectations is more insistent, and
often exhausting.

Some writers have suggested that probation officers should
be much less intimately involved in the day-to-day working of
the prison than the Home Office initially envisaged. It has
been suggested that in order to work for gradual changes
probation officers need to stand clearly apart from the prison
hierarchy and even perhaps to live and work outside the
prison buildings. This is an attractive argument, which
recognizes a real problem and suggests a solution. However,
it underestimates the loss of credibility and of sheer
usefulness, to both prison staff and inmates, which this clear
separation would entail. Probation officers ought not blandly
to disown everything that is going on in the prison apart from
their own virtuous activities. If they do, they are likely to find
themselves denied any space in which to practise; ultimately,

they depend upon the willingness of prison staff to allow access to clients. There is also the troubling argument that it is unhelpful to foster a clear split of authority into "good" and "bad" parts. Any minimally conscientious probation officer can become a "good" figure in most prisons, because prison staff get so few opportunities to be anything but "bad". The split is real and evident enough without setting up symbolic banners to announce it. Of course probation officers should recognize differences, but rather than simply proclaiming them, they need to use this awareness as a basic for change by arguing with prison staff for changes in attitudes and procedures, and making institutional processes human and intelligible to prisoners.

This line of thought sometimes suggests that the way for probation officers to improve things is to show prison staff their records of individual prisoners and go drinking with them in the staff club.[10] This is emphatically not what I am saying. Probation officers should accept and in fact welcome their marginal status in prison. The strongest argument for having people who are not members of the prison service as prison social workers is that their different allegiance enables them to remain critical, questioning, and capable of being surprised by accepted institutional necessities. This is not a very comfortable role, if you have given up seeing yourself as a crusader for truth and justice. Even when I left prison virtuously late on Friday evenings, the prison officer in the gate lodge who recorded my departure would make some remark to the effect that welfare problems obviously didn't occur at weekends. At the beginning this left me tongue-tied with guilt; later I took to arguing that prison officers were perfectly capable of dealing with anything that required immediate action, and of helping people to hang on to worries that really did demand my presence. Some probation officers in prison work a weekend rota, a supposedly conciliatory gesture which is more likely to exacerbate the resentful fantasy that only probation officers are capable of helping prisoners. On the other hand, the prison officer view of probation officers as nine-to-five men who are never around when trouble starts is understandable.

There are dangers in the marginal role I am suggesting. Probation officers may be tempted to become remote professionals possessed of esoteric knowledge and skills, a quasi-medical autonomy, and preferably some arcane technology. To find a balance between incorporation and exclusion, they must be in the prison but not of it. This means saying clearly that their business is not control, and also that they are not the only people capable of offering help. I was amazed to discover it that for a prisoner to worry about getting (or not getting) letters and visits was officially a bad thing — this appeared on the same side of six-monthly progress report forms as aggression and withdrawal. The assumption of the prison hierarchy is that the prime objective is to keep the institution running smoothly. Equally, you need actually to know the subjects of progress reports if you are to argue with the assumption, characteristic of security officers who only know prisoners on paper, that attitudes and behaviour can never change. One major difference Margaret Shaw[11] found between Gartree and Ashwell was that probation officers at Gartree saw far more prisoners because they were where the prisoners were, on the wings, not safely out of the way in the administration block or in a Portakabin outside the gate. On the wing, you are naturally subjected to a far more intensive bombardment of work. You face the hostility and resentment of prison staff openly, instead of being vaguely aware that it is around, at a safe distance. You also stand a chance of being able to change things.

Probation officers need to be where the action is; not only to argue but to listen. Prison officers are right to complain that their job is limited and unsatisfying. If probation officers can understand that discontent, they may be able to arrive to perceive of prison officers differently. Main grade prison officers are important figures in the lives of prisoners,[12] but recognition of this in the literature tends to be balanced by dismissive criticism. They are said to be just as institutionalized as their charges, authoritarian and insensitive, and set apart only by their uniforms from prisoners whose language, culture and values they largely share.[13] What this suggests is that they relate to prisoners not as parental authority figures, but as peers. The usual assumption is that this is self-evidently bad, but an alternative view might be that if this peer-group relationship could be consciously developed, it might enable prisoners to make progress by identifying with those "peers" who have worked out an accommodation with authority.[14]

Gangs always appear in the literature as malignant influences on adolescents. With juveniles and young adult offenders however, it is recognized that in practice they can be helpful too. Workers in Intermediate Treatment use the "situation of company" to demonstrate the reality and effects of behaviour that is determined by the group setting. New Careers projects explicitly use the experience of those who have "come through" to help their students recognize how they can change their responses to authority. Most adult prisoners are not in some global sense "immature", but the situations in which they commit offences often arise from a temporary reversion to a pattern of behaviour characteristic of adolescence. Burglaries may be preceded by heavy drinking in an all-male group; this in turn may have been preceded by a marital row and storming out of the house. The peergroup model of working with delinquents need not be confined to adolescents. Almost every day in the prison, I came across small things which confirmed my idea that prisoners and prison officers experienced their situation in similar ways, in particular their relationship to authority. Closeted in my office on the wing, I was unable to tell whether the swearing and shouting outside was coming from a prisoner or an officer. Directives from the prison's central management were greeted by the staff in the wing office with the same kind of angry indignation and scorn expressed by prisoners when they were confronted with a new example of authority's incomprehension and inhumanity. At the same time, in the evenings when the prisoners' work was over, I used to feel that the most positive things going on were the games of Scrabble, darts or table-tennis between staff and prisoners.

This is not a propitious time to suggest that there is an unrealized potential for creative social work in prison. Prisons are under attack and those who run them are on the defensive. Who would argue now, as Hermann Mannheim did in the mid-50s, that long prison sentences are greatly superior to short ones, because over a short term the treatment the prison has to offer will have no time to be effective? The most articulate spokesmen for the prison service, start with the assumption of failure. In the early 1960s, the story goes, a new breed of assistant Governors appeared, carrying into the prison service their social science degrees, their liberal sympathies, and their eagerness to rehabilitate those they saw as unhappy victims of circumstances. But their initial optimism was undermined by mounting criticism of prisons and the increasing volume of research which suggested that nothing made any difference and that no amount of psychotherapy, groupwork, relaxation of regimes or anything else made people less likely to offend again when they were released. Matters were not helped by the spectacular escapes of George Blake and Ronald Biggs, which led to the recommendations of the Mountbatten Report and the reinstatement of security as the main function of the prison service returned. The traditional mood of conservatism, defensiveness, secrecy and the avoidance of risks returned.

The uniformly depressed and depressing tone of the final report of the prison department's Management Review, produced in 1976, suggests that this story is true in broad outline. Its best-publicized proposal was that there should be two types of prison, one for "planned treatment", the other for "humane containment". This is not likely to be implemented, but the alternative may be one type of prison, providing "humane containment", and fulfilling, as the term implies, Stan Cohen's prophecy of prisons as "human warehouses"[15] I have criticized the 1974 discussion document but it at least envisaged the possibility of planned and positive changes; the Management Review report, by contrast, sees the main task of Assistant Governors as *controlling their staff*. The message is "Keep the lid on, don't rock the boat, the best we can hope for is that things will get no worse." The report mentions probation officers, without acknowledging the existence of research which suggests that they may actually be able to reduce the rate of reconviction for some prisoners at least.[16]

I have focused mainly on the relationship between probation officers and prison staff rather than prisoners, because prison presses so insistently on their practice. It was only after I left the prison that I realized just how heavily its burden of ordered suffering had weighed on me. Even now, in writing about the possibility of creative social work in prison, I am aware of possible hypocrisy, because I am not at all sure that I would willingly return myself. But another reason for writing at length about the environment of this form of social work practice is that I believe that probation officers are potentially in a good position to change it; not dramatically, but importantly.

I organized, with the Assistant Governor, a discussion group on the wing to which officers as well as prisoners were invited. For both groups attending meant a breach of powerful norms within their culture; for prisoners it could be seen as collaboration; for officers it meant crossing a boundary into dangerous, exposed territory. About twenty per cent of the prisoners on the wing, and two officers, used to come fairly regularly. The group was a setting in which the areas of experience shared by officers and prisoners could be acknowledged in relative safety. Each group was at times surprised by the quality of the other's understanding. The discussion group helped to keep alive some understimulated intellects, and demonstrated to the officers that the mysteries of the probation officer's craft were not so very mysterious.

It also did something for my credibility among some prisoners who had previously distrusted me — not personally, but as "the Welfare", the hypocritical promise-merchant or naïve soft touch. In an attempt to modify the attitudes of staff and to force open cracks in the institutional monolith, I tried, at progress review boards on the wing, to argue consistently for a view of prisoners which allowed for the possibility of change and took into account the fact that they had come from somewhere and would return somewhere; that they were not only or always prisoners.

Face-to-face with prisoners, I used the imminence of a parole review as an opportunity to help them research their past, explore their present situation, and set future goals for themselves. It set a context for short-term, planned work on a negotiated basis. Intensive work before writing a parole report meant that I could often make a realistic and coherent case for their release. In saying this I am not defending the present parole system; as organized at present it contradicts natural justice and can cause needless suffering. But given that one must negotiate within an established system, I was prepared in many cases to see the immediate task as simply doing what I could to get men out. If probation officers could overcome their natural deference before courts or the parole board, they would probably affect the length of sentences more than they imagine. Since the Home Office Research Unit has publicly remarked on "the potential that welfare officers have for influencing the outcome of parole decisions", they may in future feel confident enough to venture an opinion for or against in more than the reported forty three per cent of cases.[17] My experience suggests that they ought to, for their clients' sake. I certainly did not always accept a prisoner's own evaluation of his chances of success on parole. In one bizarre case,which looms large in my memory for the time I spent and the irritation he aroused in me, my main contribution to our lengthy conversations was to assure him repeatedly and forcibly, that I did not believe anything he said.

There were other men, for whom parole now or in the foreseeable future was not an issue. With them, despite some qualms about the aspects of control involved (which tended to disappear rapidly in the face of massive distress and anguish) I was ready to spend long periods discussing and developing strategies for survival, or for making their feelings of guilt and failure tolerable. I overdid this, and those (chiefly my senior probation officer and my wife) who told me to set more definite limits on involvement were right. I would quite often stay talking until nearly 9 p.m., when the prisoners were locked up for the night, covering what was often old and well-worn ground. I was unwilling to recognize the necessarily temporary, limited and provisional nature of this kind of companionship, and did not think clearly enough about the problem of dependency.

With men who were doubtful about their wives' constancy, I tried first to arrive at a realistic assessment of the situation. Where a relationship was irreparably broken, I gave what help they asked for in living with a loneliness that many of them had experienced too often before. Where there was some commitment by both parties to mending or maintaining a relationship, I tried to work with a probation officer outside to help the couple. If they asked me, I would join them on visits and try to interpret the husband's experience of imprisonment to the wife, or the wife's experience of abandonment to the prisoner. Keeping in touch with the family outside was important to maintain perspective and to avoid identifying with the view of many prisoners that all troubles come from the unreasonable and selfish conduct of those left behind.

Many of these tasks could not have been achieved as a member of the prison hierarchy. If this is true, withdrawal by probation officers would be defeatist and irresponsible, particularly since the revival of a siege-mentality within the prison service. It would amount to saying to the prison service, "You have the job of working with people who are too bad and dangerous for the rest of society to live with.

You are doing it very badly. We have tried to help, but you have been ungrateful and resisted our suggestions. We are therefore washing our hands.'' Many probation officers who have done time with enormous caseloads in desperately overcrowded victorian slums would say that it is quite unrealistic to imagine that there is any creative role for social work in prisons. And in the context of their experience they would be right: the creative potential does exist but will not be realized until we start being serious about emptying prisons. It is as well, finally, to remember that imprisonment will always be a momentous and terrible sentence to impose on anyone. Social work in prisons will always be difficult, and very rarely spectacular. But "the heart of standing is you cannot fly".[18]

NOTES

1. N.A.C.R.O.:"The Work of Probation Officers in the Welfare Departments of Prisons", 1976, p. 23.
2. Pauline Morris: "Prisoners and their Families". Allen and Unwin, 1965.
3. J.E. Thomas: "The English Prison Officer Since 1850". Routledge and Kegan Paul, 1972, p. 197ff.
4. Prison Officers' Magazine, November 1963, p. 329. Quoted in Thomas, op. cit. p. 199.
5. Quotations from a memorandum on "The Role of the Modern Prison Officer" adopted at the Prison Officer's Association Annual Conference in 1963. See Thomas, op. cit. p. 207.
6. Op. cit., p.17.
7. Julie Holborn: "Casework with Short-Term Prisoners", in "Some Male Offenders' Problems", HMSO, 1975, pp. 98-9.
8. Philip Priestly: "The Prison Welfare Officer — A Case of Role Strain", in British Journal of Sociology, Vol. 23, No. 2, pp. 221-235.
9. Op. cit., p. 94.

10. E.g. Mark Pratt: "Stress and Opportunity, in the Role of the Prison Welfare Officer", British Journal of Social Work, Vol. 5, No. 4, pp. 379-396.

11. Margaret Shaw: "Social Work in Prison". HMSO, 1974, p. 97.

12. Margaret Shaw: op. cit., pp. 43-46.

13. E.g. Terence Morris and Pauline Morris: "Pentonville: A Sociological Study of an English Prison". Routledge and Kegan Paul, 1963, pp. 98-101.

14. Cf Gordon Robb: "A Casework Borstal" ', Prison Service Journal, April 1973, pp. 7-8.

15. Stanley Cohen: "Human Warehouses — the Future of our Prisons?", New Society, 14 November 1974, pp. 407-411.

16. Margaret Shaw: op. cit., especially pp. 83-4.

17. Home Office Research Study No. 38: Parole in England and Wales, HMSO, 1977, p. 37.

18. William Empson: "Aubade", Collected Poems, Chatto and Windus, 1955.

5 "Well, then, I meet these Lunatics . . ."

NOEL DAVIES

My first experience of social work was as a child in care during the Second World War. There were thirteen in our family; my father was away fighting and my mother seriously ill in hospital. We children all went into a home, and I remember best the matron's ample bosom. It seemed to symbolize the child care service, and after that I never got on with child care officers. I went into mental health.

For five years I worked as a mental health volunteer in London, then returned to North Wales to become a nurse in subnormality. I feel embarrassed now to think of those days, yet every time I go into our victorian mental hospitals little has changed. These bastions of tradition survive, defying anyone who challenges their authority. Whole generations of staff have given their working lives in their service, and each new generation resists betraying the previous one by surrendering the fortress.

Disillusioned, I left nursing, was appointed as a mental welfare officer and became involved in a so-called rehabilitation programme — the mass evacuation of long-stay psychiatric patients from an old hospital. That was the most formative experience of my social work education.

What happened then became headlines in the "Mirror", the "News of the World" and the "People". Patients were simply thrown out of the hospital without preparation. Buses and coaches collected them and they were crammed into boarding houses, dumped on landladies. One group of patients was placed with a woman whose own children were in care. It was a travesty of a service for vulnerable, frightened people.

Why did it happen like that? The main theme of the story is politics. The experience made me realize the political implications of caring for people. Unless I took full account of that, I could never do a decent job for my clients; somewhere in that political cesspool lay the only possibilities of a better service. I had to be willing to swim in it if I was ever to help. So, ever since, I have been a political animal — an intriguer, a conspirator, a schemer.

In 1973, I was appointed Senior Resettlement Officer in Dorset. The post had been discussed for nine years. It was first suggested by a geriatrician, concerned about the growing elderly population in that seaside area, and about the demarcation disputes between himself and his psychiatric counterparts. His proposal was shelved. Revived two years later, it was shelved again. It was not until 1971 that three events simultaneously revived the whole idea. A new Group Secretary was appointed to the hospital while a local consultant psychiatrist returned fresh and enthusiastic from the Hospital Advisory Service. A Director of Social Services for Dorset was then appointed who had experience in the residential care of the elderly and handicapped. He secured my appointment — I was initially paid by the Health Service but responsible to him.

If that arrangement sounds crazy to you, it has worked very well for me. Lodged somewhere in the middle of a large organization, I would have had litle freedom of movement. My hands would have been tied by middle managers, hell-bent on self-protection. To achieve change, the best place to work is *between* organizations, not within one. I was working between two vast and impermeable giants — the old bastion of the hosptial, and the newly-created, monolithic social services. I needed to have independence and initiative to make either of them care about a group of forgotten people.

Have you ever thought of dropping out of the rat race? I recommend life in a mental hospital — preferably on the staff side. There are sports fields, dance-halls, beauty salons, bars, canteens, swimming-pools, social clubs, good food — everything neccessary for your convenience and comfort. When I went to Dorset to take up this new appointment, expectations were raised. I was seen by some as an additional amenity to make life even more convenient and comfortable. The social worker, a Penelope Keith of the social work field, twiddled her pearls and said in her best county accent, "I hear you are going to find my patients somewhere to live." No way, lady, I thought, get those pearls off and look for yourself. "Ah, Davies", said a doctor, "I'll measure the quality of your work by the number of beds you empty." Beds! I wasn't there to empty beds for consultants, or bedpans either. I was there to work with people. All such talk of beds is a symptom of the dehumanizing process of a mental hospital.

The staffing ratio in the hospital was favourable. There were 800 patients and 805 staff — one-to-one relationship! The staff included doctors, nurses, psychologists, occupational therapists, social workers, laundry staff, boilermen, maintenance men, carpenters, cooks, washers up and cleaners. Not one single person, however, had the job of preparing long-stay patients to cope with the outside world. They were there to treat patients, to nurse, feed, occupy, and to keep them alive, but not to make them readier to leave. Even I was not supposed to do that. My job was supposed to be concerned with beds. I was meant to *empty* beds in the hospital, and to *find* beds in the community. All it involved was moving patients from a bed in one place to a bed in another.

So much staff activity makes the patients aware of their sickness and helplessness, and strips them of all identity and purpose. In the occupational therapy department, patients strung together pieces of leather to make car cleaners. In another room, an occupational therapist undid them, ironed the leathers, and sent them back to be started all over again. This must be what is called cyclical care.

Part of my job involved building bridges between the different professions in the hospital. They met each other, but never really talked together, with the result that they had little understanding of each other. To get an effective rehabilitation service going, I had to persuade them to cooperate. It was no good calling a meeting — there was no precedent for such a thing. I hung my hat with the head occupational therapist, and organized a "talk-in" on rehabilitation in the League of Friends — neutral territory!

The first few weeks no-one came and we sat drinking our coffee. Then they began to arrive, in dribs and drabs. We started by trying to get each group of professionals to say what they thought other professions actually *did*. How did they perceive each other? The results were startling. No-one seemed to know and the stereotypes were stark. "Nurses", said the occupational therapists, "smoke Number 6, and sit in offices reading the 'Daily Mirror'." "Occupational therapists," said the nurses, "make dishcloths and baskets and have a sale of work, but it takes four years to train one". Doctors were either granted divine powers of healing, political and moral, or left with no role at all. What did this mean? It seemed that no profession took responsibility for defining its own skills and even when they did were reluctant to share in any real way. Is this what we mean by professionalism? We are human first, yet we seem to shed humanity with the professional cloak. This kind of professionalism fragments the patient and divides up the various bits between the groups. There was no-one who could look at the overall needs of the person, or commit himself to helping others look at the patient in this way.

The quality of care given depends partly on the quality of the interaction between professional groups. Before my appointment, a study of the hospital had been commissioned to see whether there was a proportion of the hospital population needing resettlement. Results showed that some

300 of the 800 patients did not require to be there. To my delight, the first paragraph of the report went well beyond mathematics, and focused on the behaviour of the professions involved. It pleaded for both the professions and the wider community to be more honest with each other.

My first task was to identify patients who might want to live in the community and to decide which patients should live together. In my previous hospital, the consultant just drew up lists and presented them to the staff. When asked what these patients had in common, he said, "Well, they're all schizophrenic, aren't they?" But life isn't like that. Here we let patients choose their companions. Often their choice has defied anything written on groups, but they have their own wisdom. Three rather genteel ladies chose a really tough Irish navvy. Four years later this group is still functioning happily.

These patients needed relief from the hospital regime, and their previous skills, resources and social functioning needed to be restored. Was it illness or hospitalization that had eroded these? An examination of their records revealed an extraordinary social euthanasia. Sometime — often forty or fifty years previously — they had offended some social code. In the case of women a sexual taboo had often been broken. The family and community had rejected them. The family played a role only in giving consent to extreme measures of "treatment". "Reference 1149. Date 10. 9. 48. Medical Superintendent to a Father:

Dear Sir,

I regret to inform you that your son John has become lazy, slovenly and dirty in his habits. Accordingly, I have decided that he needs a course of electro-convulsive therapy. Please sign the enclosed consent form and return it to me by return of post."

Has anything really changed since then? The nurse in our team commented, "Wouldn't a bath have helped if that was all that was wrong with him?"

Our second task was to draw up a programme offering patients a chance of daily living in the community. We changed part of the occupational therapy department into an area where skills could be practised and altered other areas of the hospital to represent the home environment. We set up our rehabilitation team — an occupational therapist, nurse and social worker to each group. It was a wonderful way to get to know the patients — working alongside them in the kitchen, washing clothes, shopping or listening to them recalling their pre-institutional life. However, we also had to recognize the limitations. None of us had had teacher training, so we could not always communicate clearly. The head occupational therapist brought in a teacher to the scheme at this stage, through the education department, and this strengthened the support system immensely. Until we acknowledge our limitations, and meet with others in an undefended encounter, we can never give a good service.

Next we looked outwards into the community. This meant looking beyond relationships and considering resources. About two months after I started in the post I asked the Area Director of Health what the budget was. He said with a laugh, "Haven't you been getting your salary?" I said I had and he replied, "Well, that's it." No budget! How exciting, I thought, no budget gives one power to run a show and means less control. As an ex-voluntary worker I knew there was a pot of gold waiting to be discovered in the community. All the money we have raised has been through voluntary organizations. The total cost to the ratepayer of resettling 253 people from hospital has been minimal.

To many social workers, the idea of resources is equated with getting more money from the public sector, and more expenditure by the big central and local authority agencies. Frequently I heard social workers say "The Department should provide it". They perceive their management as creatures from science fiction rather than as human beings. It requires imagination and initiative to raise money and interest in the community. It is creative and invigorating and stimulates new energy. It helps create a network of concern and help where clients need it.

However, it is equally important to understand and take part in the politics of the statutory agencies. We needed housing. It would have been naïve simply to write to housing officers. I knew that it was unlikely that housing for ex-mental patients would ever get on the agenda of the Housing Committee. To make things happen I needed to find out about the idiosyncracies of Housing Committees in each of the districts.

I enjoy being political, raking around in local intrigue. I became involved with all the political parties and cultivated personal relationships with the councillors. I found out who the key figures were. In one area, the Chairman of Housing was a very small lady councillor, but when she snapped her fingers, a huge officer rushed out to make the tea.

Ignorance of mental illness among local government politicians is appalling. Many councillors do not even know the difference between mental illness and mental handicap. Some feel that the mentally ill should be locked away for life. The very idea of group homes where patients look after themselves is terrifying. "They'd burn the house down. They'd rape people. They'd have orgies." These attitudes sound extreme, but they were only a different version of the kind of resistance we encountered in the hospital when first canvassing the idea of group homes. Some hospital staff were genuinely convinced that patients could not look after themselves or each other. They feared helpless passivity, not raving lunacy. "They'd lie in bed all day. They'd never wash. They wouldn't eat. They'd stay up all night."

Once one council gave a house, the rest followed. If a seaside town could give one, the county town had to provide one too. Anything the county seat could do, the first town could do better — and so on. Soon group homes were flourishing in the main centres. Persuading smaller communities to accept ex-patients was a different matter. In one isolated town we took a group of patients to meet their prospective neighbours — some friendly, others hostile. One powerful local man raised the moral issue of having male and female patients together in the same house. One of our ladies surveyed him and said, "If you're talking about sex, I gave that up years ago, and by the look of you, it's time you did too."

Finding houses was only the first stage in the battle. Resettlement schemes have largely failed to consider the whole question of day-time activities. Our team looked at day care. We did not want simply to reproduce what happened in the hospital in the community. When we had premises, the local ex-patients were invited along and asked what they wanted. They wanted something creative. They wanted to make things, but not dishcloths or car cleaners. They wanted to express themselves, and see the fruits of their labours.

The materials for our creativity centre cost money. "MIND ALIVE", (a local N.A.M.H. group) provided the initial monies, while the Social Services provided two staff, and the Health Services the premises. (This to me is a living example of true cooperation — three separate organizations linking strongly to provide a service). When we started the centre it was said that we would never get ex-patients to work unless we offered money. Because they have been offered such scope for individuality, they have never considered payment. The centre is *their* place, not ours. This also shows in the way meals are organized. They buy, prepare and cook their own mid-day meal out of their own money. Why do we pay people reward money in occupational therapy, A.T. and training centres? We do not pay a person to have a fractured arm set. If we believe that occupational therapy and A.T. training is so good for people, why aren't we communicating the benefits of it without monetary incentives?

The scheme goes on. Our rehabilitation team is still finding homes, and supporting those who have left hospital. Some patients in group homes have now been out of hospital for four years. They still need help but this can be given by unobtrusive friendly visiting, or informally at the day centre. We now have a number of active volunteers. We have a landlady scheme in addition to the group homes. We are starting to resettle residents from hostels into ordinary accommodation.

It will take twenty years to empty mental hospitals of all the people who do not need to be there. We are dealing with the results of fifty years of incompetence and neglect. How can we avoid repeating those mistakes in future?

We must be more honest with ourselves and others in the "helping professions". We spend so much time bolstering up our image as helpers, and embellishing the professional persona, that we have little time left for clients who seek our help. If we look closely, there are countless examples of how we, like some of the professionals I have described, become comfortable at the client's expense. We fail to cooperate with other professions. We neither take responsibility for our own expertize, nor do we respect theirs. We pass on people and tasks like dirty linen. We must look honestly at ourselves and see that we, like our clients, are just people, full of failings, and no better than anyone else just because we are "helpers". Only then can we realistically meet others in building a good mental health service.

Creative social work does not come out of books. Training has its value, but only as a framework. The true creative mind is one where the human spirit is not constrained, but freed to think, perceive and act to produce a better life. When professional battles end — life for many other people can begin.

Dorset had developed a combined working approach of nurses, social workers, occupational therapists and volunteers, which is not as it was, but as it is now. My sincere thanks to them all, including the Director who had faith, the consultants who agreed to differ on times, and the administrative staff who bent the rules.

6 The Child-Centred Approach to Children in Care

GWEN JAMES

THE QUIET VIOLENCE OF CARE

Occasionally, a flash lights up the dim world of "care". Those of us from the children's departments were more hardened to it than those who came hesitant and often stumbling into the "generic" departments. I believe that for outsiders — those with no experience of being in care — suddenly understanding what it is like is a conversion, a penetration of a new and different understanding.

My conversion started in 1972. A member of the department where I worked took the opportunity to spend three weeks compiling a very detailed account of the life of a boy, David, who was then thirteen. David had been in care since he was two and I had been responsible for him as an Area Officer since he was eight. I had tried to do the "right" thing. He had "broken down" in his foster home when he was eight (with screaming temper tantrums). He had then been placed in an assessment and reception centre. I had delegated the responsibility for the arrangements to one of my seniors — who was young, not very experienced and slightly irresponsible. He suddenly produced David's natural mother after a gap of six years. David had been placed in a "suitable" children's home, but continued to expect that he would

61

return one day to the foster home from which he had never emotionally separated. After some very damaging experiences in the children's home with certain members of staff, David at thirteen years old was a disastrous, disintegrated mess. For the first time — after ten years in child-care — I was brought face-to-face with the results of the sorts of decisions I was making.

For the last five years, I have been working out the consequences of that experience. I have had opportunities to listen to what the older children at last dared to tell me about how they have suffered in various "care" situations. I have been able to glimpse what it feels like to have no birthright, no claim on anyone or anything as your own as of right (everything belongs to the council); not to know where you will be living in a year's time or where you were living three years ago; not to be able to trust adults because so many have moved on that it's not worth bothering to get to know them properly any more. To learn to keep your head down so that at least things don't get worse, to have no privacy, no space, nowhere safe to keep prized possessions, and to see your friends move away and have no power to keep in touch.

In speaking to some colleagues about these glimpses I am rated as emotional, over-dramatic, too involved and unprofessional. The only people who understand are those who have had a similar experience. Any creativeness in the work I and my team have done has been inspired by these insights into the isolation of children in care.

In 1971 my area team in North London was responsible for 400 children in care. At the re-organization into social service departments, five child-care officers stayed in post but by 1973 they were beginning to leave and the new social workers coming in were enthusiastically embracing the "generic" approach. I either had to allow the children in care to be allocated to generic social workers (who worked under the extra pressure of not quite knowing what they were doing most of the time) or I had to find an alternative way of offering a service. As a result of the autonomy given to me as an Area Officer and a sympathetic boss, I was able to gradually convert one of the team sub-groups to a Long Term Care Group (L.T.C.G.). These social workers only work with children who are growing up in care. Gradually the idea took shape, helped by an able group of supporters from outside the department (this group was to develop two years later into the 'VOICE OF THE CHILD IN CARE'). I acted as senior of the group as well as being the Area Officer.

We all had heavy caseloads. We cut every corner; our recording was patchy, but somehow we survived and laid the foundations of work with these children. The rest of the department was actively hostile, especially when we tried to move the group out of the area team to become a centrally based resource in 1975. We eventually achieved this and were able to take responsibility for about 200 children. Because the team has no other pressures or responsibilities, it is now possible to give a more concentrated service to the children, especially these who are "isolated". This term describes those children who are out of touch with their own families and who have not been placed in another one.

We aim to provide, through a team approach, an opportunity for children to build up relationships and some sense of trust. Social workers undertake to stay in the job for at least three years, so that there is some continuity. We encourage the children to develop a sense of their own worth so that long-term planning for their future can be built upon it. Long-term planning will include family placement whenever possible, and in some cases a return to the child's own family. We have successfully placed many older children with a previous history of difficulties and disturbance. In order to find suitable homes it has been necessary to place some children at a considerable distance and the members of the L.T.C.G. travel a great deal.

In the case of those older or more difficult children for whom family placement is not possible, the group aims to improve the quality of the child's life. The aim is to identify for each child at least one "reliable caring adult" — a person who is significant and who can take a personal interest in him. Whenever possible this should be someone outside the department but sometimes the only "parenting" available is through the sustained interest and support of members of the group itself. Such children and those identified as being at risk of becoming "isolated" are taken on camping and youth hostelling holidays each year so that they get to know several members of the group quite well. There is a close liaison with residential workers and in some cases they are identified as keyworkers for children. If a child has to move home it is regarded by the group as similar in effect to a major surgical operation.

In 1972 I bought a large house in the borough to use as my home and to provide a residential resource. For the first few years it was run by a very competent girl who had previously been in care, but since then I have run it myself with occasional help from friends. I have had up to six young people living there and often have eight or nine at weekends. I have the house for two reasons. First so that I am able to offer sustained help to children when they are going through a crisis period (it is impossible to offer this in a short-stay residential resource where there are staff working on a rota basis). Secondly, I have been trying to work out ways that "isolated" children can be "parented" within a local authority. Social service departments are given "parental rights" over children but little thought is given to how the "parenting" can be done. Through the experience I have had with the L.T.C.G. and the use of my house I have begun to develop some practical ideas. Without a residential resource of our own I am sure we would not have been able to help so many "isolated" children on the road to independence. The young people who have most needed this help are boys at boarding school who have lost their "home base" and boys of fifteen, sixteen years old who have had to move from their foster home or children's home.

It is quite untenable for a field social worker, who appears infrequently and then usually only when there is "trouble", to have a major responsibility for making the arrangements for the life of a child growing up in care. Somehow we need to combine the authority with physical care in the same way that a parent does. The person or people with the responsibility for the child should be part of his life, someone who is either helping to care for the child or who at least is based in the same building. This is the only way that really makes sense to the child.

For some reason it is considered "unprofessional" for a field social worker actually to live with children in care. There are murmurings of "role confusion" and the dangers of emotional involvement. I have often felt sorry for the young people who have come to my house, usually as a last resort, because of the strong feelings most of them have had about social workers. To them it must have seemed like the final degradation to actually have to live with one.

ANOTHER CHANCE FOR JOHN

The responsibility for John (aged eleven) was passed to the L.T.C.G. from an area team because his social worker was offered a place on a training course at the last minute. She told us that John was not happy in his foster home, that she had not really been able to get to know either the foster parents or John during the year as their social worker (she was the third in three years!). She thought that the situation might break down. The first week that we had the case John stole some money from a teacher at school. His new social worker from the L.T.C.G. brought him back to the office and he then came back to my house while she went to have a talk with the foster parents. John had said that he was scared to go home because he would be hit. The foster parents found his stealing hard to cope with but they wanted to struggle on. He returned to their home later that evening. Two days later he was discovered acting dishonestly at school again and ran away. He went missing until 11 p.m. the following evening and by this time the foster parents had decided that they would not have him back. He had been with them for three years — his previous foster parents having been unable to cope with persistent bed-wetting and stealing. Until he was five he had lived with his parents before they separated.

John was found at a police station on the other side of London at 11 p.m. at night, hungry and dirty. Because of the foster parents' decision he had lost all the familiar life that he knew. He already had serious problems and he was only eleven. Who would want him and what would become of him? He was potentially another David.

In the same way that an intensive care unit in a hospital is available to offer immediate and massive support in the case of severe physical injury, the L.T.C.G. was able to offer help which John needed. The social worker and I had agreed that if he was found during the night I should go to the police station to fetch him (she lives a long way out). He had already been to my house so he came back to a place that he had visited at least once. He knew that there was no question of returning to the foster parents because the police had told him of their decision. It transpired that in the long run he was relieved not to return. He came home with me and stayed for five weeks until he moved to live with a young couple as his "permanent home". His social worker saw him nearly every day and had him to her home for two week-ends. He was able to continue at his own school (with a few ups and downs). The social worker tried to help him to piece together his past and to make some sense out of it.

While he was with me I tried to help him build up a sense of worth and of positive hope for the future. I could not leave him on his own at all because he lit matches and played with fire. He stole money from several people in the house and office. He could cause chaos very quickly. He was not popular with the other boys in the house. He had rather a "little gentleman" look about him which did not fit with their tough "punk" attitudes. It was a great strain (not least because of the mountains of wet sheets) and I thought longingly once or twice of the short-stay children's home which is where he would have been in any other circumstances. I felt a great need for social work support myself and for someone to help me, quite separate from the person who was helping John. However we all survived and I took John and all his worldly goods to join his new family. He had met them twice previously once at my house and had had a weekend with them. They are both teachers with much experience of youth work and strong links with their church. Friends from the church who already foster two older boys for us had put them in touch with us in the first place. They had been assessed and approved by their own Local Authority.

What chance is there of this placement working? John is attractive to look at, he has a zest for life, he is interesting and interested and he is young for his age. The young couple have waited a long time for a child and they have been told about John's problems. Things will not be easy but the alternative for John is a life of institutional care. He went off as "patched together" as his social worker and I could make him. He did not go through the insecurity of an assessment centre or a short-stay children's home. He was not exposed to a group of children in the same state of insecurity and anxiety as himself, many of whom can be unkind and aggressive. He did not have to meet and get used to seven or eight residential staff as they came on and off duty. Our work was child-centred and for those five weeks John took precedence over practically everything else for both of us.

At eighteen years old David has recently gone out of care. He lived in a boy's hostel from the age of fourteen to sixteen when he moved out because of his aggressivenes. He was in a bed and breakfast hotel for over a year and then given a bed-sitter by the Housing department. He has survived — just — but the damage is deep. He gets no fun out of life and is lonely and withdrawn. If we had been able to offer him a better service when he was eight years old, the course of his life might have been different.

Each child in our care has only one life to live. Our policies and practice must somehow be changed so that we can treat each one as an individual and develop the most suitable plan to meet his needs. What happens at the moment is that children are put through a process which is convenient administratively but takes little account of their feelings, or need for security and stability.

7 Social Network Assembly

ROD BALLARD and PETER ROSSER

In recent years an increasing array of therapeutic methods has informed social work. These include reality therapy, transactional analysis, gestalt therapy, conjoint family therapy, and so on. Each method expounds its theory and practice in books, pamphlets and articles. Students and staff on social work courses often find themselves under pressure to "know something about" a wide range of methods without having practised them in a systematic way. Pressure of work drains away the energy to think creatively about the various different types of intervention. Today, social work lecturers may not have opportunities to practise although they are likely to know something of the academic content of different methods through reading professional literature. For lecturers practice is not written into the job description, so any practical work is likely to be seen as extra to an already heavy teaching load.

All this makes it difficult to try out new methods systematically. The way things are organized simply does not help problems of motivation and the excitement of ideas which are a necessary prerequisite to the risk taking involved in actually *doing* any of these approaches. Sitting down with a client and conducting, say, a transactional analysis, may mean the worker will be behaving in totally unaccustomed ways. His usual strategies, his tried and tested approaches will be replaced by strange and new ways of working which may fundamentally alter his familiar role in the eyes of clients. It is extremely unlikely that he will be supported by supervisors with knowledge of the method.

We decided to try out one particular method of intervention — social network assembly. The idea began when Rod Ballard came across the work of Speck and Attneave while preparing a sociology course for social work students on family and kinship. It was developed in tutorials with one student, Peter Rosser, who rapidly became fascinated with the idea of networks and the effect and impact they have on individuals. Peter had recently experienced being part of a large family gathering which had taken place some months before he joined the course. He had been involved in quite intimate and different ways with some of his own relatives and this experience was fresh when he came across the idea of network assembly as a method of intervention. We think that this is important, because one of the problems with doing anything new and experimenting with different ideas concerns the area of motivation and taking risks. In our case it involved quite simply reading a book, trying to relate it to our own personal experience and then going out to try the method mentioned with a real family and its network. We had to overcome our own personal apathy and quite considerable anxiety at the prospect, and it is probable that we succeeded in this because we could identify and link our own personal experience with that of a group of people in trouble.

As a method network assembly involves bringing together in one place as many friends, relatives and neighbours of a person in need of help as possible. The first requirement is that a suitable client or family can be found to agree to cooperate in the venture. Some examples from the literature include a one parent family,[1] a schizophrenic girl,[2] a malfunctioning North American Indian Network,[3] an acute psychotic,[4] a patient suffering acute paranoia,[5] a widow suffering from anxiety and reactive depression,[6] and a patient suffering from nervous breakdown and inability to cope.[7] So far clients with a mental health problem have been the main group undergoing the process of an assembly with their networks. However, there is no reason to suppose that the idea could not be tried out with other client groups.

The method attempts to achieve what Speck and Attneave call the "network effect". This is a kind of turn-on phenomenon of complex group interactions which stirs people to new relationships, removes unhealthy binds and allows the growth of constructive resourceful bonds to hold the network together. New network structures of friends and relatives may "evoke the potential capacity of people to solve their own problems as an antidote to the aura of depersonalized loneliness characteristic of post-industrial society".[4] The idea is to lay open family privacy, to loosen intense negative emotional binds and to create practical resources to overcome such things as physical isolation, work and recreation difficulties, loneliness and so on.

Bringing together large numbers of people in this way can be a fraught and difficult business. There are often kinship rivalries and jealousies, neighbour disputes, problems with employers and other agencies, marital and other difficulties, all concentrated together in one room. People may feel guilty about not having done more to help others in the network. They may feel angry that they themselves have been let down at times; frustrated by unsuccessful attempts to offer help; or rejected when they have asked for it. It is not surprising, therefore, that we had considerable anxiety about organizing such an assembly. We had no experience of bringing people together in this way, let alone "conducting" the scenario once it had been set up. We tried the idea out with a role play comprising all the students in Rod's class on family and kinship, and this gave us considerable confidence. The exercise generated much enthusiasm amongst the students, who took part in a very creative and helpful way. A kind of network effect was in fact generated, which had useful spin-offs, because it helped people to get to know each other (it took place early on in the course) and gave us a live opportunity to examine both the possibilities and problems with the method.

The next stage was to find a suitable referral. An important requirement here is that the client for an assembly should be selected at the point at which he is in need of help and is at crisis point. Garrison[8] suggests that the social network should be used in a crisis because "people are often far more amenable to change and allow a caregiver to promote positive growth in brief periods of time". Clearly members of the network must also feel that the situation is serious enough to warrant their attendance at the meeting and exposure of themselves and their private lives in front of so many people. We waited for our initial referral until Peter started his first course fieldwork placement in a local social services department. Having obtained the cooperation of his supervisor he kept himself in readiness for a possible referral and towards the end of this placement an isolated family with problems centred around an eighteen-year-old girl called Christine emerged as a possible candidate for the method. After an assessment of their problems we decided to go ahead and try the idea out with them.

Christine was living at home with her mother, father and younger brother. The mother was becoming so exhausted with the situation that the family G.P. felt she was verging on a breakdown. Christine was unable to hold down a steady job and her problems included outbursts of temper and violence towards members of her family, her workmates and friends. She was said to be unreliable, uncooperative and generally impossible to live with. The problems of the family were aggravated by the fact that they were living in an extremely isolated tied farm cottage.

Christine had been admitted for a short period to the local psychiatric hospital following a violent episode in the old people's home where she worked as a care assistant. The family was known to the hospital social worker and was also on the caseload of Peter's supervisor who had been unable to do much to help them to get to grips with their difficulties.

Peter was asked by his supervisor to intervene after yet another incident in which Christine had attacked her brother.

Social network assembly requires a team of therapists, led by a conductor. They work closely with him, their main task being to support and identify with network members who are vulnerable, to sustain the group interaction, and perhaps to help with the strategy of polarization of attitudes in the group when and where this is appropriate. This last process can involve attempts to get people to say what they really feel about each other and this can sometimes take place when sub-groups form — for example, when members of different generations voice differences of opinion about what is appropriate behaviour in a given situation. The role of the assistants here might sometimes be to work up feeling, in order to get as open and honest communication as possible.

We wanted to follow closely the guidelines set down in Speck and Attneave's book and that meant recruiting some other people to form our team. Peter's supervisor, Jonathan, had been interested all along in our ideas and he readily agreed to take part, together with the hospital social worker who knew the family as a result of Christine's admission to the hospital. We also asked a student, Christy, who was close to Peter to join us.

For about a fortnight Peter prepared the ground, by involving the family and the intervention team in the idea. None of the family had any prior knowledge of Speck and Attneave's work and neither did two members of the team.

The family were asked to invite all the guests to the house of the local vicar on the appointed evening — their own family home was unfortunately too small. Peter awaited replies and followed up two neighbours who refused to come. After experiencing their anger and despair, he felt that these feelings should be expressed openly and persuaded one to attend the assembly.

The team met twice before the first assembly to work out the roles the team members would play and to stipulate the goals of the network intervention. We agreed for instance, that Peter was to chair the assembly, having practised with two student groups using role plays. Rod was to act as catalyst — raising and lowering the tone of the meeting as necessary — and was to be in charge of tape recording. Christy was to support Christine and arranged to meet her socially with Peter before the first assembly.

The goals of the network intervention were twofold. First, we wanted to form a viable social network around Christine to give her support in leaving home and finding employment, and to increase her opportunities for making social contacts with her peer group. Second, we hoped to rekindle the network that surrounded the parents which had become so unhealthy and unsupportive so that other people could share the burden of Christine and her brother, who was also liable to have temper tantrums. It was decided to try and achieve these goals in one or two meetings.

On the appointed evening we arrived early and installed the tape recorder, placing the microphone in a clearly visible position. We waited apprehensively as Christine's parents welcomed the guests into the vicarage until eventually there were over thirty-five people in the living room, with every chair taken up. The social network included the "client family" of four, twelve relatives of both generations, four ex-school friends of Christine with whom contact had been lost, the matron of an old people's home where Christine had once worked, several neighbours and friends including the vicar and his wife, and the intervention team of five.

When we had obtained consent for recording the assembly and stated that everything would be completely confidential, Peter briefly explained the difficulties facing Christine and her family, expressing the belief that those present could, and should, be able to help if they were prepared to change themselves. Physical encounter group techniques were not used because none of the team were experienced in this field and there was no room to move about in any case.

Everyone was involved from the start. We asked each person to say in turn what he or she knew and felt about the problems of Christine and her family. Looking back we feel this was a mistake because it took each person's focus off himself and on to Christine at a time when we wanted everyone to think about their own behaviour and how they might change it to help Christine's family. It might have been more helpful to start by talking about people's own feelings at being part of such a large group and what expectations they had of themselves.

Christine found being the focus of attention too stressful and after ten minutes she walked out, never to take part again. We had discussed the possibility of this happening, and of her not turning up at all at a team meeting, where it was decided that her presence was not vital for the achievement of either goal, especially the second. Having observed the reaction of the assembly we continued the meeting. It was decided that one of the network would follow her and make sure she got home all right.

The first stage of the discussion contained a lot of anger against Christine, especially from the neighbour mentioned previously and the matron of the old people's home. Some members tried to justify their failure to help the situation, some enjoyed the amusement of the network members over their tales of Christine's bizarre behaviour, while others claimed that Christine had been quite normal with *them*.

As the anger exhausted itself, people seemed to become depressed, perhaps because they realized that they hadn't really done much to help Christine. Nothing positive was brought forward and negative feelings predominated. We allowed these feelings to continue for some time and then called a break for tea.

People collected into small groups during the break where we hoped positive ideas might be formulated. Team members met individually with Peter to assess the situation and to plan how we could introduce some possible solutions later in the meeting if nothing happened.

Soon after we started again offers of help did come forward, the most plentiful coming from the matron who had previously been very angry. People offered help with accommodation, employment and transport. The meeting ended on a businesslike note with Peter committing people to various offers of help they had made. We agreed to meet again in three weeks time. We left the meeting feeling uneasy — Peter felt he had said too much and pushed too hard, perhaps because he felt under strong pressure to make a success of the exercise. The team hadn't really seemed very united, and had found it difficult to collaborate on one train of thought.

One team meeting was organized between the two assemblies but only three of the five members attended, which perhaps reflected the feelings mentioned above. Interestingly enough, only about three fifths of the first assembly attended the second meeting — along with two cousins who hadn't been able to attend the first gathering. At the team meeting we decided that our task for the second assembly was to concentrate on the support network for the parents because we knew that despite geographical propinquity, the extended family had failed to visit the parents for many months.

The second meeting began with a relaxed gathering of the network where family photographs were swopped and the latest family gossip was heard. This stage is called "retribilization" by Speck and Attneave.[4] It was soon noticeable that various significant people hadn't arrived. The powerful matron failed to appear and never got in touch again. (Some months later she was found guilty of embezzling funds from the old people's home and was sentenced to a term of imprisonment!)

We began by discussing what had happened over the last three weeks and the mother described how she had told Christine in detail what had happened at the first meeting, and believed that this had had a good effect on her. Apart from a minor outburst of jealousy, Christine had been pleasant and cooperative in the household and was going out with a young man. Peter's supervisor pointed out that such improvements had occurred in the past but had not been maintained.

People were asked what contact they had had with Christine's family over the last three weeks, especially those who had made specific offers to help. It was noticeable that some members of the extended family who had been most verbal at the first meeting had not subsequently bothered to get in touch.

Focusing on this point, the intervention team finally "gelled" and cooperated sensitively on exposing the communication breakdown within the network. We began by looking at what kind of help network members could provide and several offers were eventually made. However, it was clear that network members didn't offer help readily and that the parents had never readily sought help. Network members said that they hadn't been aware of the seriousness of the situation, especially the state of Christine's mother. It was equally clear that mother, let alone being unable to ask for help from her network, couldn't even ask for it from her husband. Father felt she "worried too much" and that Christine would "have to sort herself out". As the focus of the meeting fell on father he became more evasive. He tried to refocus the meeting onto Christine, and stated that "if you professionals can't do anything about it, how can we?" Perhaps a transcript of part of the tape best illustrates the evasiveness of father and the difficulty the network had in helping itself.

Peter: I think there's something wrong with your relations to your family, friends, neighbours, and relatives if you cannot ask for help.
Father: Yeah, but the point is, if you've got trouble in the family like that you don't like to go to your neighbours or your friends and get them involved in our troubles. That's my trouble.
Peter: Why not?
Peter's supervisor: But you go beyond that don't you? (You

involve) the social services and the police and it's getting bigger and bigger.

Father: (Refocusing on Christine) When she (Christine) went in there, she was ......

Rod: But wait a minute ...... Do you think it's easy to ask your relations for this kind of help? ...... Now, it's a very difficult thing to ask for help, because asking for help makes you feel inadequate and not a very good parent (a loud yeah from mother) ......

Mother: (Going back to Christine) I think all the talking's been done, I think she'll just alter within herself now. (Aunts nod in agreement)

Peter: (to Aunt) No. What do you think about the reasons that mother and father cannot ring you up or write to you and ask for help? ......

Aunt: Why they can't? I don't see why they can't. They could if they wanted to.

Peter: Why do you think they don't want to?

Aunt: Perhaps they don't want to involve anyone else.

Peter: But they do because they involve the police, they involve public people, they involve social workers.

Aunt: You don't know other people's minds do yer? (This is her sister!)

Second Aunt: I suppose they thought you were more qualified.

Psychiatric Social Worker: Oh we aren't.

Peter: I don't think that's in fact the answer. Are you embarrassed to talk to your own family and say "I can't cope any more?"

Father: (refocusing on Christine) No. The point is you see, that matron, when her (Christine) went down there ...

Peter: Forget about Christine ... Look, mother has been very near breakdown with what's going on with Christine. Mother, you must admit you've been in a terrible state about Christine.

Mother: Oh sometimes I have.

Peter: Now all I'm saying is, she was in this state, you weren't able to help, the social worker etc. weren't able to help, why couldn't she get her family to help? ...

Father: Well it's like I said before, you don't really run to your family to get your family involved?

Peter's supervisor: Why do you think that?

Father: Because when she (Christine) started on the doctor ....

Peter: No! Not Christine, we're getting back to Christine again. Why can't *you* go to *your* family and ask for help.

Father: Well, I don't see that they can do anything about it.

Peter: But if mother is just feeling tired, worn out, exhausted — can't take any more, why can't the family help more?

Rod: ... For instance, one of the things mother could do would be to say "I've had enough, I want to come and stay."

Third Aunt: We've got a spare room.

Second Aunt: She can come with us any time.

Mother: Yes, well I know I could.

Peter: Why haven't you then?

Mother: (very quietly) 'Cos my duty is to stay home and look after them.

Father: You don't have to stay home and look after us. We can manage.

We never did actually find out the underlying reasons why the network hadn't been offering support. However, it was clear that the communication difficulties over offering and asking for help, as shown by the network as a whole, were reflected in the "client" family itself. This much we did get clearly into the open and it was both encouraging and exciting to see very definite and real offers of help coming forward as a result. It began to feel as though the network was collecting around mother especially, in a supportive way, and there was a euphoric feeling of breakthrough and happiness in the room. This was similar to what Speck and Attneave call the "exhaustion-elation stage" in which all involved leave one another feeling tired but with a sense of having worked hard and done something positive to help, and even perhaps with a feeling of completeness and satisfaction which has been missing from their lives.

In their account of the assemblies which they have conducted, Speck and Attneave describe how the therapy team leave the room inconspicuously to let the network find itself, unhindered by outsiders. In our second session we made a deliberate effort to leave in this way and succeeded easily. This would have been quite impossible at the first meeting, since people were still tentative about each other and needed support from the team till the end. Apparently, it was a long time after we left the second session that network members finally went their separate ways.

One of our most vivid recollections of the experience is of our "escape" to the pub after this second session. We were well and truly into the "exhaustion-elation" syndrome. We felt a sense of success, almost of euphoria, at what had been achieved. Clearly, relationships between the intervention team network had also changed — from being competitive, sceptical and apprehensive to being mutually supportive, relaxed and relieved. We were close to each other at this point — a feeling which arose out of a sense of "humaness" and personal regard. We felt that we were equal and participating members of the human race. We were involved with the assembly because of any statutory authority we had or possible power we might wield, but because of a desire to try out a new idea which was totally unfamiliar and experimental. We wanted to help families which were stuck, in a way which was real.

While there was little tangible evidence that much had changed, we did feel that people would be more supportive and helpful towards each other within the network. No social work involvement followed the last assembly but Peter's supervisor followed it up with a visit ten months later. He discovered that after the network intervention, Christine had obtained employment without help but that another hysterical outburst four weeks later had led to a further five days in hospital. On discharge, she returned to work but had to give it up for medical reasons. Since then she has been unemployed and living at home for seven months. She was found to be more communicative and showed interest in a retraining programme. During Christine's period in hospital and the following months the network were involved in a supportive role. Her mother remarked on the fact that she heard from or saw relatives more frequently in those ten months than she had done before our intervention.

Relating back to the original goals of the intervention it appears that our first goal of forming a viable social network round Christine was not achieved, although she now seems to have a more positive attitude to her own future. The second goal of reforming a supportive network round her parents was achieved. This is demonstrated by the way in which the family and its network were able to get through the crisis of Christine's admission to hospital without resorting to help from police or social work agencies.

In our example, some people came together to experience an excitement of ideas which motivated them to try something new and refreshing. The split between the academic institution and the field was bridged for a short while. Yet, when it was all over the people involved went their different ways. Peter and his fellow student left the course. The supervisor's contact with the university fell off because he did not have another student. The band of professionals who were involved together in such an exciting way ceased to exist.

People within organizations are sustained and motivated to work by colleagues with whom they can identify, in whom they can trust and who know them well. There are structural problems in working *across* the boundaries of organizations, which involve the basic human need for support, encouragement, a social identity and sense of belonging. We felt that our involvement in the network, and the personal risks to which we exposed ourselves, arose not from the encouragement of those around us but from within ourselves. Our colleagues were interested, but we did not continue to work with the idea and try it with different families and in different settings. Clearly our motivation was not strong enough. The argument here is thus that the system of ideas and beliefs which organizations generate are what motivates the individuals within them to function in their professional roles. When they operate across organizational boundaries these forces are not so effective and fail to sustain the cooperative activity which has been the concern of this contribution.

Sometime afterwards, a seminar was held with social workers and those professionals who had taken part about the network assembly. We were struck by the apathetic and frankly discouraging atmosphere. We played some edited tape recorded highlights of the assembly and in the ensuing discussion most social worker colleagues seemed unimpressed, suspicious and not particularly enthusiastic. It was not so much that they were critical of the method of intervention (although, not surprisingly, many of them were) but that the collaborative style of the exercise seemed to go unnoticed. One would expect this response in the current climate which is inimical to the excitement of ideas.

This lack of enthusiasm can be explained in other ways. Speck and Attneave note the fragmenting effects of rapid social change on the networks of individuals. Rapid social mobility, the destructive effects of urban "planning", with slum clearance, high rise flats, the development of new housing estates, ably documented by writers like Young and Willmott, "create new tensions and precipitate distress that should not be interpreted as a guise for old pathologies". Taking the adolescent condition as an example, these writers say that "clinically, adolescents seen today are simply not the same as the youth of past generations. They appear depressed and hopeless, but they admit rather than blame themselves. They see the world situation as hopeless, and they are hungry — but for dialogue, not therapy. They are suffering from real distress of the soul, and so are their parents, teachers and peers".[4]

Talking with social workers and students about our attempts to make a tiny impact on these forces has been a salutary experience. There is fear of doing "damage", of using too many "resources", of simply taking the risk. The lack of follow up and of any attempt to replicate the method locally seems symptomatic of a social condition which equates with Speck and Attneave's depressed and hopeless adolescents. This is not surprising, if we follow their model. Overnight, our social services suffered two major upheavals, first by the creation of Seebohm departments and then through local government reorganization. This disrupted the networks of thousands and created a bureaucracy which has immobilized and crippled the creative drive of members of the care professions.

It is not a question of laying blame but of recognizing what is happening. We have all become victims of a social process which forces us apart from each other, which undermines the responsibility we once had for our fellow human beings and which makes it extraordinarily difficult for us to entertain an excitement of ideas which should be the stuff of social work training and practice. There are ways of combating these forces by using network assembly as a method. It is a question of risking oneself and one's clients and of joining forces with them in a cooperative effort to fight the processes which are creating such distress and humiliation for so many thousands of human beings.

Against the background of these ideas it is not surprising to find that we have made little attempt to follow up the outcome of our involvement in the network assembly form of therapy. What has happened is that our *own* networks, which we created together, have become fragmented. The links which we formed as a therapy team were not strong enough to bind us together and the attempt to develop and test a theory of helping dried up almost before it started. The excitement of ideas which got us going originally was not sufficient to sustain the work, and we sank back into our traditional stylized routines.

NOTES

1. R.V. Speck: "Psychotherapy of the Social Network in a Schizophrenic Family", Family Process, 1967, Vol. 6, p. 208, p. 214.
2. R.V. Speck and U. Ruevenie: "Network Therapy. A Developing Concept", Family Process, 1969, Vol. 8, pp. 182-191.
3. C. Attneave: "Therapy in Tribal Setting and Urban Network Intervention", Family Process, 1969, Vol. 8, pp. 192-216.
4. R.V. Speck and C. Attneave: "Family Networks", Pantheon, New York.
5. J. Garrison: "Network Techniques. Case Studies in the Screening-Linking-Planning Conference Method," Family Process, 1974, Vol. 13, pp. 337-353.
6. R. Cresswell: "How Mrs G. Built up a Winning Pack", Community Care, 12th January 1977.
7. R. Cresswell: "Peter, A Suitable Case for Treatment", Community Care, 26th January 1977.
8. J. Garrison: op. cit.

8 Memoirs of a Long-Distance Tightrope-Walker

BILL JORDAN

I have been a social worker for fourteen years. For ten years I was a full or part-time probation officer, followed by four years part-time from a psychiatric hospital, all in the same area of Devon. Creativity has been only one element in that experience, and sometimes outweighed by frustration or despair — but it has been a necessary ingredient. Without it I could not have developed or persevered.

I am aware of a number of polarities in my social work practice, which have emerged as ill-concealed contradictions and paradoxes. For instance, I was simultaneously both the local probation officer and the secretary of the claimants union. However, these contradictions have contained creativity. Social work can and should engage the passions — in my case, it has especially evoked a commitment to the needs and rights of underprivileged people. Equally it often demands a kind of self-discipline which is more subtly creative. It also requires persistent goodwill towards intractable and unresponsive people. In my case, it has involved an unexpected loyalty and devotion to one small and slightly uncouth community.

My own social work motivation partly stems from political ideals about what society should be like, and the role of the Welfare State. I believe that social work should try to give its best services to the most disadvantaged and deprived people, and those who are specially disturbed and destructive. This is

85

not an obvious recipe for creative work. It often means working with people who are mistrustful, and sometimes with people who are extemely hostile. It raises problems of power and authority, of coercing people into doing what they do not want to do. But I believe that social work cannot avoid involvement in these unpleasant dilemmas without being largely irrelevant to the lives of those who most need help. In other words, it should never seek to be creative by being selective in a self-protective way, either in terms of its tasks or its clientele. In my view, social work should primarily be a way of giving certain personal services which are essential to a welfare state, and not a means for developing the therapeutic skills of a group of professionals, however gifted they may be.

However, there are unquestionable greater dangers in the practice of statutory social work than in other settings. Both the agency's power and the clients' vulnerability maximize the possibilities of doing harm. I have always been very conscious of the risk of making people worse, even by uncritically accepting their invitation to "help" them in some apparently innocent way. I am very conscious of mistakes I have made over the years, and have tried to learn from these mistakes, both by acknowledging them to myself and admitting them to clients.

Ever since my early days as a probation officer, I have been concerned to try and combine empathy with realism. I often felt under strong emotional pressure from clients to do something to "help", which afterwards led to disaster for them, or to a false and destructive relationship with me. The pressure stemmed from my feeling for the client's fear or pain; but this caused me to ignore some equally important aspect of his situation and of my role in it. The problem was how to remain aware of these other factors and to stay realistic, without seeming harsh or insensitive.

Over the years I have learnt to be quickly and vibrantly aware when such a dilemma is approaching. For me much of what is creative in these encounters is the sense of the risks involved — the dangers of losing my balance. It feels like walking a tightrope, where one slip will cast me and the client down into the abyss. This sense of danger causes the adrenalin to flow; every word and gesture seems important. This is obviously an overdramatization, but it seems better than false complacency. In the past I have made mistakes through pretending that no danger existed, though lulling myself into believing that I could safely follow where the clients led, or by allowing myself to be swept along by my own feelings. The crash would come later.

An example from my recent experience illustrates some typical dilemmas, and my own style of trying to keep my balance. Three years ago, a seventeen-year-old girl called Tania was admitted to our hospital, following a suicide attempt. She came from a disrupted family, had been abused by her parents, and rejected from an early age. She had been educated at a boarding school (after being assessed as educationally sub-normal), and since leaving school had led a Cinderella-like existence as a drudge in residential establishments in various parts of the country. She was a closed-in, self-hating person; yet she was attractive and had a lovely smile. She took a kind of perverse delight in frustrating efforts to draw her out or increase her sense of worth, and I spent many frustrating hours, both while she was in hospital and for many months afterwards, listening to her negative brooding. Nonetheless, she placed a high value on the hospital, and especially on one doctor, Dr. Allen, and to some extent (more ambivalently) on me. Thus, it was no great surprise when she returned there two years later, determined to make better use of its facilities after another bad patch. Indeed she was a lot more positive and responsive, and in the process met another patient, Bob, aged thirty-two, recently widowed, whom she shortly married. She then went to live with his three children.

The following interview occurred only three weeks after she had left hospital to start this new life, for which she was so ill-prepared. I had arranged to visit Bob and Tania at home, and see them together. When I arrived fairly late in the evening, Bob went to make coffee, and it was immediately clear that Tania had a lot on her mind. She poured forth an account of how her elder sister's two children had been burnt to death in Scotland, how this had not been an accident but pure negligence on her sister's part, and how awful she felt about it. She wept as she showed me photographs of the children, and my heart went out to her, as I knew how she must be identifying with both them and their mother. As she raged against her sister, I realized how much her own self-image as a newly-created stepmother must have been shattered by this tragedy, and I wanted to try to tell her that I understood her conflict and her pain. Yet the moment Bob returned with the coffee, she launched into bitter criticism of him, saying she only married him because she felt sorry for him, for the sake of his children, and because she wanted a child of her own — but he could not give her a child because of his vasectomy. I froze with sudden awareness that Tania could not hold on to the hurt of her sister's tragedy, and was turning all her feelings onto Bob in an orgy of blame and hate. But this was not all. After a few moments of scathing reproach of him, she turned on me and Dr. Allen. She said that we were the only people she could trust; she had no faith in Bob. "And it's all your fault really, because you got me to trust you." So now she turned to us as her *only source* of help, and demanded to return to hospital.

Pausing at this point to analyse my dilemma is like holding one frame of a fast-moving film. There was really no time to think as Tania hunted first Bob and then me, as if we were clumsy animals. Yet as she spoke I saw the bear trap she had made for me. It was my understanding, my empathy — the feelings I wanted to express for her plight — that made me the trusted person. But to be the trusted person was to usurp her husband's role, to reinforce the division she was making between her bad new marriage, and the love and trust she felt for Dr. Allen and myself, whom she had known for so much longer. In the act of showing compassion, I was inviting her to regress, to revert to the safety of being a patient, from the terror of being a wife, a stepmother and a "normal person".

So I said, remembering that my medical colleague had been to their wedding, "Well, if you feel like that Tania, why didn't you marry Dr. Allen instead of Bob? He was there." As I had hoped, Tania the huntress stopped in her tracks, and looked a bit thrown. Then she said that I must know that wasn't what she meant. Surely we wanted to help her. She had always believed that she had a special relationship with Dr. Allen, and that he could really help her. I acknowledged this feeling of hers, but wondered whether it was really help she was asking for. I reminded her what mixed feelings she had had when that sort of help had first been offered, and how often she had rejected it. I told her that she could be using Dr. Allen and me and the hospital as a stick for bashing Bob, and that I wasn't prepared to become so trustworthy as to undermine the marriage. She scathingly dismissed her marriage, and wrote Bob off as a pitiable failure as a husband. When he tried to defend himself she brushed him aside. She would sleep with any man who would give her a child. She should never have left the residential home where she had worked, or Siegfried (the superintendent) who had been her lover. In her heart, she still loved him. I said to her that it was obviously far better to be Tania the Cinderella, dreaming of pumpkins and coaches, waiting for her Prince Siegfried to come and sweep her away. (My imagery got a little mixed in the heat of the moment.) Tania retorted angrily that I seemed to be saying she was looking for a father figure. I replied that it was a fantasy figure, a fairy godfather. The question was, could Tania live in the real world, and give up her fantasy suffiently to be an ordinary person, with day-to-day problems. As Tania suddenly looked calmer and more reflective, I felt able to say that I recognized how terribly hard this was for her, especially as the death of her nephew and niece reminded her of her own childhood, her fears that everything she did went bad; that she would never be part of a happy family group. Tears came to her eyes. In a different tone of voice she said that she was no good for Bob; she should leave him or kill herself.

I had finally reached the hurt and despairing side of Tania that she felt unable to share with Bob. I wanted to allow her to express some of this, and to get some response from him. I had felt uncomfortably aware of his passivity up to then, and also that I might seem to be "taking his side". I was also aware that I knew him much less well than her, so I could not measure his investment in her reactions. At this point, however, he did make a positive contribution, and said that he felt that Tania was always trying to prove something — either that she wasn't a bad person, or that she was a very bad person. She tried too hard to prove herself. Tania said no-one believed in the bad bits of her, no-one accepted they were there. I said quite firmly that I did, and reminded her that she had asked me to tell Bob about them when they first met, and that I had slightly shocked her by doing so, in detail, in her presence — though Bob had shocked her more by accepting them.

Tania switched again and became bitter against Bob. She said he only pretended to accept her, and that he was more interested in everything else than in her. Bob pointed out that Tania made it very difficult for him to go to work. At this she threatened to kill herself and sleep with another man if he left her alone. I said I didn't think she'd be able to do them in that order, and Bob added, "That's the trouble with Milltown, there aren't many necrophiliacs about". She then accused me of laughing at her. This gave me the chance to say that I was really deadly serious and that I was very concerned that she would damage herself and her future by throwing away this chance of a new life without really giving it a try. I could see only too clearly why it was difficult, why it hurt to try and be normal, why family life was painful and problematic, and how her sister's tragedy made it all doubly hard. I could also see why she tried to get me to "help" her undermine all her own best efforts. Perhaps in the end she would leave Bob, but I was not going to be the one to accomplish it for her then and there. I would pass on her message to Dr. Allen, but I would also pass on my own. Tania became very angry. What was the point, if I was going to make Dr. Allen see it my way? She said she was furious with me and Bob. I suggested that she and Bob would have a lot to talk about when I was gone, and would find it easier if I left immediately. I asked her if she ever wanted me to come again. She said, angrily and emphatically, "Yes!" I said I would come again in four weeks, and I expected that Dr. Allen would see them both in the intervening fortnight, on an out-patient basis. As I left, Tania gave me one of her rare smiles.

I have tried to indicate both the excitement and the risks I sensed during the hour or so this interview lasted. It reflects something of my own personal style of coping with what I felt was, if not a crisis, at least a "crunch" — a crucial test, from which future patterns would take shape, both between Bob and Tania, and between myself and them. Obviously, much is lost in the telling, and if my words sound rather harsh or brutal, I hope that I conveyed non-verbally the goodwill and concern I felt. At the end, I had a feeling of creativity. It came from a sense that Tania was beginning to feel a truer emotional response to her distress, that she was actively fighting her way out of the corner I had put her in; and that Bob was also reacting more positively. I was thus envigorated by recognizing that they had gained some strength from what might have been interpreted as a cruel and painful confrontation. This seemed more important than preserving a false and potentially destructive image of myself as a nice, helpful, understanding and trustworthy person.

There seem to me to be close parallels between this kind of work and many of the most difficult situations faced by social workers doing statutory tasks. The dangers are alarming — children damaged or killed, suicide or homicide — but they can act as a spur. While the feeling of panic is oppressive and disabling, the edge of fear can be exhilarating. Panic causes the worker to overreact, to be swamped by real or imagined dangers, or alternatively to lose touch in the opposite way, by reassuring himself and the client quite falsely, denying and obscuring all the danger signals. Both over-reactions and under-reactions are uncreative, because they lead to a loss of real contact between worker and client. A balance between empathy and realism allows the worker to take risks, and to acknowledge with the client that he is doing so. It allows the kind of honesty and directness that is refreshing for both parties — looking anything that is wrong straight in the eye, but also by recognizing real strengths and potentialities. The client experiences the respect and freedom of being treated as he is, and is neither baulked by authoritarian constraints, nor cossetted with cloying sympathy.

I have concentrated on this one example because it illustrates how I find a creative element in what is otherwise exhausting and difficult work. This is the creativity which is available somewhere in most of the unpleasant statutory work that social workers do. It lies in the search for ways of sharing constructively with clients the very nasty and unpleasant aspects of one's feelings and one's role. It is not comfortable to be investigating a non-accidental injury, or deciding whether to compel someone to go into a mental hospital. It can only become in any sense creative if both parties find a way of telling each other their personal truths. So often in social work we feel confused and unreal — we doubt our perceptions, our emotions, our judgement. Yet we still have to decide and to act, frequently against the wishes of those we are trying to help. Unless we can find ways of communicating to clients what they do to us, and hence our own reality, we can become imprisoned in a nightmare world, in which we intervene, monitor or control people whose lives do not touch us, and who are not touched by us. We become unwilling and lugubrious spectres that haunt our clients, always frustrating but never helping.

I am aware of the dangers in my particular style of working. I have an insidious tendency to become covertly hooked on my own strengths in crises, my ways of resisting pressures to do harm to my clients. Unless I am careful, I can find pleasure in these rather dramatic situations, which encourages clients to enact them for me. I can also become very isolated, and create an impression of being the only source of strength and help. I make my own hell of overwork and unrealistic demands by being too reliable, and by implicitly cutting clients off from other sources of help. My best remedy for these weaknesses is to work closely with others — specially those in other professions who offer quite different kinds of assistance, in different settings. In the example above, I was tempted to visit Bob and Tania again the following week, but felt it wiser to let them see Dr. Allen next and return a month later. This proved to be the right kind of formula. They have survived the subsequent year, and are beginning to settle into their marriage.

There are many other ways of breaking out of the straitjacket of meaninglessness and muddle. My experience with the claimants' union convinced me that the support of a group of people who have experienced similar troubles is often as effective as the kind of social work I have described — but in a completely different way. The creativity of such a group comes through a kind of instant mutual trust that takes a social worker years to cultivate. People let their defences down and become open to help as soon as they recognize the real acceptance that such a group can give. If social workers can play a part in the formation of such groups, they are doing something as creative as years of work with individuals and families. If they are as fortunate as I was in having an opportunity to participate in such a group, they will experience the exhilaration and excitement of an entirely different way of helping.

In addition I have found the continuity of working in and being part of a smallish community an extremely creative aspect of social work — the community consists of a town of about 20,000 inhabitants and its surrounding area. Social workers often talk about the community, but they seldom live in it or stay in it or get involved in it sufficiently for their clients to see them in anything more than their professional role. Over fifteen years my clients have tended to bump into me on Saturdays, and on market days, or to have been fellow-members of the claimants union or the sports centre. We have read about each other's cricketing or footballing triumphs and disasters in the local paper; we have been to the same parks, cinemas and picnic spots. We know the same people, the same places; we have local events and landmarks in common, and our children go to school together; they damp-proof, paint, wire and plumb my house, they fix my car; I help them sort out family and social problems and occasionally give them a hand in their gardens.

What is the value of all this in strictly professional terms? Well, it means that much of the artificiality, the formality and the stiffness of most social work contacts is simply not there. I know of them and they know of me before we ever meet; we can place each other in a context, in a network. It is easier for me to see their immediate troubles — however bizarre and spectacular — against a background of what is ordinary, sane and natural in their lives. They see me as part of their locality, not as the representative of another culture. I don't feel that this stops me being focused, disciplined and therapeutic, but it does stop me being unrealistic, partial and omnipotent.

One example may serve to make the point. Fred and Francesco Endicott were the twin products of an evening's encounter between their mother and an American serviceman. Brought up by loving but ineffective and rather elderly foster parents, they ran wild in their youth, and when I first met them early in 1965, Fred was in Borstal. He is the most inarticulate person I have ever encountered, making up for what he lacked in vocabulary by a facial expression of such guileless candour that it largely excused his total irresponsibility and ineptitude. Once, when his car ran out of petrol he was pushed along the motorway by six policemen who never noticed that the car was untaxed, and that Fred had neither a driving licence nor insurance. Francesco tried hard to look after Fred; he was always marginally more capable and law-abiding but made up for this by his exploits with girls.

It is hard to summarize the years I have known them, or to select from all the contacts — social, family and professional — I have had with them. Fred's period of Borstal after-care was distinguised by crises of every kind, worried visits to my office and home by Francesco, shaking his head and furrowing his brow. Fred had to battle — almost to the courts — to win consent to marry a farmer's daughter, and I was involved in negotiations with irate parents as well as arrangements for the wedding. When Fred got into debt a few years later, he came to me for help again. When he and Francesco set up as window cleaners, mine was the first house they attempted — the bucket slipped from Francesco's nerveless grasp, and drenched Fred from head to foot. Francesco was a member of the claimants union, and distinguished himself by doing a silly dance in front of the television cameras when we were trying to film a serious news item about our allotment scheme.

Then, Fred's marriage broke up — his wife lost interest in him when he settled down and got a steady job, and she ran away with a delinquent cousin. He arrived at my house late at night, weeping and heartbroken. For months, Francesco and I helped him put the pieces of his life together again, pay off his debts, get custody of his daughter. Now he has remarried and is a father again, an active member of a church, and a pillar of society.

To my amazement however, Francesco turned up a few months ago as a patient in my ward of the mental hospital. At thirty-five he had had one affair too many, had got hopelessly entangled with a twenty-year-old, had left his wife and four children, tried several times to kill himself, crashed and written off his car, and largely lost his business. He was quite unable to talk about this with doctors or nurses, but his inhibitions melted away at the sight of me. He soon wanted to go back to his family, but there was a great deal of work to be done to repair the relationship between him and his wife. With support from Fred, he began to be able to take a painful look at himself, and I am now involved in some quite ambitious work with both of them together. My long acquaintance with Francesco has not stopped me using such artificial techniques as sculpting with him and his wife, nor has it inhibited me from involving him in art therapy — indeed I doubt whether anyone else could have got him to do either. But it does enable me to say "come off it" when he shoots a line, and means that he will laugh out loud, instead of being hurt or angry. I can be much tougher with Francesco than my colleagues could be, but I can also recognize the lovable, generous, dynamic clown in him much better than they could; I know that he was a good father, and that he probably will be again; I can see so much more than the burnt-out Lothario that he presents to other people. Incidentally, he lives a few doors away from Tania and Bob, and they are friends. Francesco and his wife, Tania and Bob all come out with a group of other ex-patients to the pub with me once a fortnight. Fred and his wife are going to come too, when the baby is a little older.

9   Clients as Social Workers

MARTIN SEDDON

For the last twenty years, an increasing number of former offenders, ex-psychiatric patients and clients of social service agencies have been getting jobs as social workers. The schemes which promote this process are known collectively as New Careers. This essay considers some of the factors influencing this trend and looks at the distinguishing characteristics of a New Careerist's relationship with his clients and his professional colleagues.

PRINCIPLES

The main principle behind New Careers is to use people who are the products of social problems as agents of change. Amid mounting concern about the effectiveness of conventional social services, it has been claimed that a great deal of natural talent within clients is being wasted. The bold aims of this philosophy were summed up by a Californian director of community services in 1967.[1]

New Careers can serve a vital purpose in meeting coming manpower needs, in helping us adapt our human services to those most in need of them, and in providing career opportunities for those now left out of the desirable employment market.

Traditional social service agencies, particularly the larger ones financed by the state, have often been criticized for

97

failing to provide an effective service for the more alienated groups in society. With mounting workloads, the social work and income maintenance services have adopted increasingly defensive postures. Their staff tend to come from middle-class backgrounds, removed from the daily life experience of clients, and they operate on the basis of treatment models that isolate those they wish to help in a dependent role. The centralization of their offices means that staff are less aware of feelings within the communities they serve and less likely to use or develop indigenous support systems. Many of the needy are deterred from approaching these agencies until they become desperate. Ineffective preventive services mean that people fail in ways that are seen to require drastic corrective measures, such as imprisonment or mental health treatment, with a consequent cost in both human and economic terms.

By contrast, the comparative success of self-help groups (which emerged particularly in the 1950's and 60's) in serving those same sections of society has not been widely publicized. Groups such as Alcoholics Anonymous, tenants associations, lonely hearts groups and weight watchers have vital elements that state agencies lack. The warm welcome to new members, the directness of communication and the positive sense of fraternity and identity are very important to those in need. The crucial factor in these groups is that all members are participating in a shared helping process. Even the most unstable individual can contribute to the welfare of other members and gain personal satisfaction which helps him set further objectives for himself. The numbing distinction between helper and helped, embodied in the practice of the official agencies, is replaced by group and individual dignity and support. Of course self-help groups have disadvantages, particularly their instability and patchy geographical coverage, but they set standards against which conventional social services should be judged.

New Careers attempts to draw on the lessons of the self-help movement. In particular it advocates the recruitment and training of those who have first-hand experience of social problems to act as agents of change both in their employing bodies and in the communities they serve. Their knowledge of the receiving end of official social services motivates them to press for new social policies. Their familiarity with the cultural setting of clients enables them to relate more directly to individuals and their problems, and to intervene in a way that will encourage client participation. New Careerists become involved with their clients on the basis of a shared attempt both to identify and understand the causes of these problems, and to develop constructive methods of response. Being relatively at ease in the world of their clients and able to relate to the machinery of officialdom, they provide the missing link between the agencies and those they were designed to serve. It was anticipated that New Careerists would have a contagious effect in two areas of their work; by exposing professional colleagues to new styles of intervention and by motivating their clients to emulate their achievements.

EXPERIENCE IN THE USA

The idea developed in the United States in the 1960's when the growing instability of inner city areas became a political issue. Within the context of increasing national wealth there were ghetto areas in which the symptoms of social malaise — unemployment, disease, crime, illiteracy and mental breakdown — were increasing. The state welfare agencies were making little impact because they could not recruit sufficient staff and had styles of operation which were designed with a more willing and compliant consumer in mind. Imaginative responses to these problems were encouraged and the Kennedy administration made considerable funds available.

In 1965 two educationalists, Dr. Arthur Pearl and Dr. Frank Wiessman, published an influential book entitled "New Careers for the Poor".[2] It drew on the experience of numerous small ghetto projects over the previous ten years which had employed indigenous people to make contacts and open up lines of communication. The talented workers used by these short-term schemes could not be retained to make a permanent impact on social provision. Pearl and Wiessman promoted the concept into the arena of large-scale agency policy and met with a favourable response from the interested parties: the politicians saw it as a way of reducing the numbers of potentially troublesome unemployed; administrators noted that New Careerists would be cheaper to employ than professionals. Reformers saw New Careers as providing creative work for those who were typically discriminated against, and expected that it would result in more effective services for clients. The established professional social workers gained least from the idea, which had grown from a critique of their own service, and it is significant that the innovative work was undertaken largely by educationalists and psychologists.

For offenders, the first demonstration project was started in 1965 by a Californian prison psychologist, J. Douglas Grant. Two years earlier he had called a national conference of self-help groups at which ideas for a New Careers training programme had emerged. He then selected eighteen men who were nearing the end of their prison terms and who, despite considerable criminal records, were thought to be capable of turning their own vivid experience of social problems to practical use in the welfare field.

The style of the training, which was also influenced by the work of Dr. Maxwell Jones (who had used many kinds of non-professional staff as "social therapists" at the Henderson Hospital in England), emphasized the value of training group members to help each other understand their personal experience, rather than adopting external theoretical solutions. After an intensive course which lasted four months the participants were paroled and most of them secured employment in the social services.[3]

Men and women have risen from the ranks of these early

new careerists who now hold important positions with responsibility for the deployment of large-scale services and funds. One, who is currently Deputy Director of a government agency responsible for young offenders in a large state, was instrumental during the early 70's in framing the policy of decarceration of young offenders in Massachusetts. Another has played a prominent part in designing new roles for para-professional workers in a national mental health agency. At grassroots level it is now quite common for state or charitably funded social work agencies to employ a significant proprotion of ex-clients.

DEVELOPMENTS IN BRITAIN

Observers of the American social work scene began to popularize the New Careers idea in this country during the early 1970's. However, there was not the same political urgency here to experiment with new types of social service. Statutory social work was still enjoying broad support for its increasingly professionalized methods.

Against this background the National Association for the Care and Resettlement of Offenders (N.A.C.R.O.), working through its Bristol branch, sought funding for a pilot project. As a pressure group for penal reform, which managed limited social work enterprises itself, N.A.C.R.O. was aware of the shortcomings in social work provision for offenders and wished to see New Careers extend some of the boundaries. However, the only agency willing to fund a pilot scheme, the Home Office Probation Department, did so for rather narrower reasons. It was concerned with the limited effectiveness of Borstal training and was prepared to fund a New Careers scheme provided that it could be shown to be an effective way of dealing with young adult offenders. The Home Office remains uncommitted on the wider implications of New Careers.

Since early in 1973 the Bristol New Careers Project

(B.N.C.P.) has provided a full-time training course in practical social service which lasts twelve months. It has the capacity to take up to twelve students who are selected according to the following criteria: they must be between seventeen and twenty years old; they must be awaiting sentence at a Crown Court in the South-West and likely to be sent to Borstal; they must be motivated to work with social problems; they must be of good intelligence, and must not have severe personality problems. The training has three components. First, there is practical work experience as staff assistants in a graded series of social service placements (such as youth clubs, schools, day centres and hospitals). Secondly, there are classroom activities aimed at helping the students to learn from their placement work. Third, there are various types of groupwork and individual counselling, at the residential centre, to help them achieve greater personal stability.

The bulk of the training and the running of the hostel base is supervized by three New Careerist staff. Known as "Linkers", these are ex-offenders in their mid-twenties who have had some previous social work experience. For the time being the project is coordinated by a probation officer but naturally it is hoped that a New Careerist will be employed in this capacity when one emerges with suitable administrative abilities.

The success of the B.N.C.P. has been less spectacular than the drafters of the original proposal anticipated. They had spoken of "significant numbers of potential social workers currently in the Borstal system" but the project has only identified about five per year who wish to take up this work at the end of their course. (Pro rata this would be about 30 per year if the facility extended its catchment to the whole of England and Wales.) Nonetheless the project has continued to enjoy the backing of Home Office officials in terms of their own criteria and a recently published account of the first two years work identifies some of its related achievements in providing a setting in which personal growth can take place.[4]

The employment of ex-offenders in staff roles as Linkers at B.N.C.P. has been a notable success. Although some were appointed mistakenly and had their contracts terminated prematurely, half have gone on to university courses, two have become professionally qualified social workers, and one is now a regional training officer for a large charitable social work agency.

The development of additional New Careers projects in this country was restricted by cuts in social service budgets at a time when planners were beginning to show an interest in the idea. However, three other schemes did receive funding in the early 1970's. The Barbican Centre in Gloucester employs two New Careerists in key positions in its comprehensive social training facility for probation clients. The Alcoholics Recovery Project employs New Careerists to manage a shop-front help centre and three accommodation units in South London. The Hammersmith Teenage Project employs six New Careerists in its programme of community-based alternatives to care or custody for local juveniles. In 1974 other similar projects were shelved but in recent years the Probation Service has taken advantage of Manpower Services Commission funding to sponsor New Careerist posts both in residential work and in various forms of fieldwork.[5]

The scale of development in this country has not reached that in the U.S.A. There is no coherent national policy and individual New Careerists remain isolated from each other. The reasons for this appear to be rooted in our methods of administration. In this country, the majority of the national social service budget is administered by the main statutory agencies. Our charitable sector lacks the scope and financial backing of its equivalent in the U.S.A. and it is not capable of promoting the same degree of experimentation. Although directors of state financed agencies have expressed cautious interest in New Careers, there has not been a sufficient variety of successful pilot projects to convince management that investment of scarce funds in this way of working is justified. In the meantime, ex-clients are obtaining employment in a piecemeal fashion by competing for standard social work jobs against other applicants. These workers have then become concerned with the removal of barriers to their advancement within the system rather than creating a separate New Careers hierarchy. (One university has recently informed candidates for professional social work courses that experience of being a client is considered an advantage.)

I would now like to take a closer look at how the theory of New Careers works out at an interpersonal level. What are the special features of a New Careerist's methods of work? What effect does he have on his professional colleagues? What problems does he face in achieving a new personal equilibrium in a demanding role?

Most of my observations are drawn from my experience of working closely with ex-offender staff members as director of the B.N.C.P. for three years up to February 1978. I shall be using the male gender to the New Careerists (N.C.s for short) because the residential duties seemed to deter suitable women from applying for staff vacancies. I am aware that some other schemes have had positive experiences with female ex-offenders, particularly former prostitutes and drug addicts.

STYLE OF WORK

The interpersonal transactions between an N.C. and his clients are characterized by sharing of experiences and ideas. This contrasts with the more usual "treatment model" in which a "qualified" practitioner either does things *to* his clients (thus converting them to *objects*) or *for* them (thus making them dependent).

The N.C. stimulates thought by offering his own experiences as material for his clients to examine. The skill lies in presenting this in a way which encourages clients to explore possibilities with him that they have either discounted or just not thought about before. This joint process can be separated into three stages: problems that have been common to both parties are established; insights with these problems are exchanged and developed; purposeful methods of response to them are explored. The issues dealt with in this manner could range from controlling violent impulses to obtaining fair treatment from a landlord.

The first step in this process, the personal encounter between client and N.C., can be quite dramatic. Suddenly realizing that there is something different about this "man from the Welfare" can creatively disrupt defeated minds. The weekly selection meetings at Bristol illustrate the point. Groups were arranged at the local remand centre for up to ten young adult offenders together with one or two of the project's N.C. staff (Linkers) and myself. The majority of these youths would receive Borstal sentences when their cases were eventually dealt with, and the dull routines of the prison together with the demands of the inmate subculture had reinforced their defeatism. In public they were defiant, and blamed others for their predicament, but in private they were depressed and confused.

Faced with this stagnant situation, the Linkers would often articulate a blunt challenge such as: "*I* sat where *you* are until I decided to get off my fucking arse!" After the silence had been broken the Linkers would exchange views and reason with the group, but the youths we spoke to at subsequent selection interviews (the ones who had indicated that they wanted to talk about their future) often said that it was the personal confrontation that had started the process in them. The image before them of an ex-con, complete with tattoos and authentic street language, being dealt with courteously by the prison staff and influencing decisions that would be made about their own lives, clashed with their view of the world. Being confronted by such a person, who had been one of their own kind, implied the question "If *he* can do it, why can't *I*?" This penetrated to a deeper level than professional reasoning would have done.

However, this transaction has complications. We all use

various people on whom to model parts of our behaviour and have ambivalent feelings of admiration and resentment towards them. If negative feelings took the upper hand in the remand centre group, the youths would accuse the N.C.s of "selling out" and therefore being "worse than the screws"; at best they must have "conned the system" and were still "one of the boys". At the other extreme, there was a danger of creating naïve optimism in those who wished to deny serious personal problems. However, and indication that the message had hit home might reveal itself in a chance remark that could easily be missed: a youth might take a long look at the fading tattoo showing beneath the new Levi shirt and then ask rather pensively, "They wouldn't have the likes of *us* working in a youth club! ... ... would they?"

Long-term involvement between an N.C. and his clients continues with the process of establishing mutual issues of concern in greater detail. The N.C. will observe and relate with his client in a variety of different settings and then begin to concentrate on situations that highlight issues which either party thinks are particularly problematic. This is illustrated in the following extract from a case record written by one of the Bristol Linkers. It concerns a new student who had a gambling problem:

I was in the kitchen on Saturday morning with Tony. He was studying form in the newspaper, picking out the horses he would bet on when the bookies opened. We got talking about feelings and he described the building up of excitement, the apprehension and good feelings he got when the bookies opened and he was in there. I then described how I used to feel when I was waiting for the chemist to open so I could pick up my herion prescription. He drew some parallels.

A second example is taken from an internal report prepared by an N.C. staff member on another student;

Gordon could easily become violent. I spent a long time trying to get him to realize what he was feeling before a violent confrontation erupted. I did this by telling him about myself, how I felt in pubs and discos and how when I felt like this it was likely that I would get into a fight, but that now by being aware of what was happening I could avoid trouble and control the feelings. Once again I wasn't trying to get this guy to suddenly stop being violent but to be more aware of what was happening below the surface of most fights, and by becoming aware he might be able to control the situation and avoid getting into trouble. I also let him know it was hard for me and something I was still working on.

The spoken part of this transaction began with a series of low-key exchanges of thoughts and feelings whilst the two men were actually in the pubs and discos. Interspersed with a good deal of pub talk and general conversation, there would be leading observations from the N.C. such as "That makes me feel really small", when a girl refuses him a dance, or "I wish I didn't feel I need to make an impression here," when entering the local pub.

The final stage in this process involves the learning and adaptation of social skills that will lead to a more purposeful management of problem situations. N. C.s have consistently favoured methods of shared learning that involve role-play, simulation, critical incident analysis and related techniques. These methods have recently been catalogued by Phillip Priestley, a research worker who has been a consultant to N.C.'s schemes for a number of years.[6] In the case of the aggressive student, Gordon, a number of role-play sessions, jointly undertaken with friends, colleagues and a drama therapist helped him to identify methods of avoiding confrontation whilst retaining his dignity. Another student N. C., who was working with persistent truants in their own haunts, recorded on video their reasons for absence from school. He then began recording the theories of their teachers with a view to using the tape to start a joint meeting that would take a fresh look at the problem in the school. Unfortunately he left Bristol before this was completed but involvement in this gap between schools and their more wayward pupils has continued to bring out creative ideas from the students. Other common interest groups, such as local tenants or those who consistently fail to secure employment, find satisfaction in using rehearsal techniques to develop new strategies. The task of the N.C. is to help the group achieve the confidence to share experience and to be sensitive to group feelings.

This style of work is extremely demanding at a personal level. It means that the N.C. must expose his thoughts and feelings to an unpredictable audience who at times may, for their own purposes, take delight in treating his weaknesses with ridicule. The path he is inviting his clients to take begins with the abandonment of inbuilt cultural denials that offer consumers temporary protection from indignity and misery. Although the N.C. will be motivated by his personal emergence from the client role, his effectiveness will also depend on the backing he gets from colleagues and management.

AGENCY CONSIDERATIONS

The nature of his relationship with the other staff of his employing agency will greatly influence an N.C.'s security and effectiveness. Often he will work in a setting in which there are few guidelines and with problems that the agency has not previously tackled. He will be in closer proximity to feelings of anger and despair in his clients and will be exposed to extreme forms of deviant behaviour. However, the support which he needs from his colleagues will be impaired by feelings that his presence evokes in them.

The barriers between professional social workers and their clients are considerable. There is consternation if a client goes into a staff tea room but when one of them legitimately crosses the boundary and becomes a colleague, ways of redrawing the boundary may be found to ensure that he is still excluded from complete equality even if he was a client of another agency.

An example of this phenomenon, involving the current B.N.C.P. director, illustrates the difficulty we all have in accepting N.Cs into our fold. The following exchange took place at a staff meeting shortly before a very reliable and long-serving N.C. colleague was due to take up a university course in social work;

Staff consultant: How do you feel about Terry leaving?
Replies: Sorry. . . . I don't know how we will manage.
Staff consultant: Any other feelings?
Project director: Hmm ... ... I suppose I'm glad in a way. He's getting too professional.

Terry perceived two meanings in this comment. One was that in some ways he was seen to be getting out of touch with his roots and becoming more difficult for his clients to identify with. But, the primary message, as the director then confirmed, was to do with a professional social worker's feelings of discomfort when an N.C. starts to play the professional role. N.Cs are seen as an asset, perhaps, provided they stay in their place. Another example was brought home rather forcefully to me after three years of an apparently fruitful working relationship with ex-offender staff.

I was discussing draft sections of this essay with a former N.C. colleague. I was rather stunned at his observation that I was seeking differences between a N. C.'s methods of work and my own in order to feel safe. He had never lost the feeling in our work that I was maintaining a barrier.

A rather more dramatic example of this differentiation occurred early in my involvement with the B.N.C.P. I had invited someone who was noted in professional circles as an authority on residential work to discuss some problems in the project's hostel with the staff team. After delivering a lengthy and self-justifying initial exposition he invited reactions. Billy, who had stopped listening early on, rounded on him with the comment, "You sound like the kind of person who talks loudly in restaurants without knowing what the hell he's on about.'' Billy was obviously feeling "de-skilled" by the "professional", who in turn had felt the need to justify himself to those whose credentials were gained from first-hand experience. Another common defensive strategy involves placing the N.C. in situations that are removed from the mainstream of the agency's work, where he is expected to achieve miraculous results with little support. While this may be rationalized by pointing to the need to give his new skills space to develop, it is hard to avoid the conclusion that the inevitable failure is not received with too much sadness on the part of the "professionals".

A satisfactory response to the emergence of former clients as partners in a new enterprise must take account of the realistic concerns of both parties. Established staff will be worried that N.C.s may revert to previous forms of deviant behaviour; that they may collude with their clients and compromise the reputation of the agency by using risky and unconventional methods of work. For their part, N.C.s will fear that their professional colleagues may wish to restrict their use of experimental styles and make them adhere to unimaginative bureaucratic procedures. They also fear isolation from colleagues and lack of access to management. If the outcome is to be desirable constant attention must be paid to staff dynamics (the B.N.C.P. staff team had additional fortnightly meetings with a psychiatrist to facilitate this) and there must be a commitment from management to keep agency aims under continual review with the staff.

A closer and more flexible relationship between staff and management is required if the latter is going to give realistic support to N.C.s. The unconventional locations and unusual working hours make effective management difficult. Becoming a social worker involves the N.C. in a number of profound personal changes. He will already have made a tentative commitment to a new set of values but during the transitional phase he will be earnestly seeking, and deserves to get, comprehensive feedback from colleagues and management.

PERSONAL ADJUSTMENTS

All of us experience difficulty when establishing ourselves in a new role. However, the problems which face an ex-client when he begins working in a social service agency are more complex, and if he is an ex-offender these can be particularly acute. The step he is taking involves both the reorientation of attitudes towards institutions which have previously regulated his behaviour and changes in personal relationships.

Being a client of a social service agency usually induces hostile feelings which show themselves in general suspicion of the agency's staff. When an ex-offender becomes an N.C. he has to cope with feelings towards probation officers, prison officers, the police and social security clerks which have often been formed in moments of conflict. One of the Bristol N.C. staff said that the thing he disliked most was "striving to become acceptable to people I don't really like, but who I know I need to get on with in order to benefit me in the future and do my job properly."

Adjustments in work relationships, however, seem to be made relatively easily compared with the problems that are faced in restructuring private lives;

When I go back home I feel alienated from my old mates and their way of life. This used to bother me more in the beginning about two years ago but as I have grown within the job I feel more confident and stronger about who I am and where I am going. In the early days, though, I was easily hurt by some of the sly remarks they made about me being a probation officer now, and I must only be doing it for the money, or that it was a cushy life. I found it hard to understand the intense jealousy and resentment I picked up as I still considered myself as one of them and I liked to be thought of as one of the boys. I was also scared, as their way of life still held a great attraction to me and I felt I could get more instant gratification than I was getting at New Careers. People still remembered me as a tough guy and I liked the way they looked up to me and feared me. It was the opposite in Bristol. I had to work hard at getting people to accept me for who I was and what I had to offer and not the heavy image I used when I was on the street.

That quotation highlights the difficulties faced by an N.C. who needs to keep in contact with the good parts of his old life without compromising his current position. The experience of most New Careers schemes is that this conflict is a major cause of termination of employment, greatly outweighing shortcomings at work. Damaging relationships from the past can be held over by some as an insurance policy in case failure as a N.C. reccessitates re-entry to a system that feels safe.

In rebuilding new support structures N.C.s noticeably draw strength from their clients. Even though the sharing process, is risky and demanding, it allows for greater personal feedback. At the B.N.C.P. there were important occasions when, as in Alcoholics Anonymous, the weakest student supported the strongest staff member at a point of personal crisis.

CONCLUSION

There is a creative appeal in the notion of the helped becoming the helpers. Given proper planning and suitable styles of management it has been shown by a small but growing number of demonstration projects, that ex-clients can make an effective contribution to social work provision. In a rather isolated way N.C.s are beginning to work out their concept of involvement with clients. Agencies or individuals who are thinking of starting a new scheme — whether it would involve full-time posts or simply using ex-clients in a voluntary capacity — would be well advised to discuss their proposals with those who have already gained some experience of the problems involved.[7]

However, New Careers does not simply attempt to provide individual solutions to the problems of a few lucky clients who manage to obtain social work jobs. It expects that the styles they subsequently adopt, and their influence on agency policy, will benefit some of those in need who are not being reached by existing strategies. It is more difficult to say to what extent these broader aims can be achieved in this country. The majority of our N. C. are still employed in low paid, low status jobs where their efforts attract little publicity. Apart from the few demonstration projects, the jobs that they have secured were not set up with N.C. in mind and the temporary nature of the Manpower Services posts means that the impact of the ex-offender is limited. Those who have progressed to positions where they could have more influence are only beginning to get established and it is too soon to judge their likely impact.

NOTES

1. Burton Powell, summing up a New Careers conference in Los Angeles, April 1967.
2. Arthur Pearl and Frank Wiessman, "New Careers for the Poor." The Free Press, 1965. Available from Macmillan, London.
3. A more detailed account of this project can be found in "New Careers for the Disadvantaged" by Nancy Hodgkin. Published by N.A.C.R.O., 125 Kennington Park Road, London S.E.11, price 65p.
4. "Another Try: An Account of a New Careers Project for Borstal Trainees" by the Dartington Trust Research Team in *Alternative Strategies for Coping with Crime* editor Norman Tutt, Blackwell, 1978.
5. In the three years to December 1978 the South Yorkshire Probation Service has employed 34 ex-offenders on twelve-month, full-time contracts.
6. Priestley, McGuire, et. al., "Social Skills and Personal Problem Solving — a Handbook of Methods." Tavistock, 1978.
7. The N.A.C.R.O. Information Office can provide some suitable contacts.

10   You Can't Win 'Em All

PHILIPPA SELIGMAN

In this chapter my aims are to describe who I am, and to say what I do and how I feel about it and how my "clients" react to me and my work. The inverted commas are there because although I accept the use of the word "client" as a convenient label for consumers of a service, it is not an appropriate word to cover all the people with whom I work, either within my full-time job or outside it. The line between helper and helped, teacher and learner, giver and receiver is a wavering one, constantly changing in position and in strength. "Let me help" and "Help me" sometimes sound the same. Recognizing our own needs does not make us weak — it makes us more sensitive and stronger. I played the encounter game with some students recently where your partner keeps asking you "Tell me who you are?" I've played it many times and a chapter this length wouldn't contain a fraction of it nor bring me or you nearer to the final truth about who I am.

It is not that easy to describe what I do either. Let's start last Sunday. A student called Andy had written to me on behalf of a voluntary emergency student counselling service called "Nightline". He had heard about encounter groups and sensitivity training groups and thought the Nightliners could benefit from such a group. Some friends who belong with me to an on-going growth group agreed to join us on following Sunday evening at the student union. I didn't know whether to expect six or sixty but in the event, only three of our group turned up and four of the Nightliners. Andy had booked a large common room so we made an enclosed area with chairs, sat on the floor, examined our socks, wondered whether our feet were smelly and whether anyone else was feeling apprehensive.

After some preliminary chat with the group about their worries that Nightline wasn't being used enough, we started to discuss how difficult it is to make meaningful contact between strangers. We began to do some encounter exercises round this theme. First, we went round the circle. Each person said his name, and accompanied by a gesture expressing how he or she wanted to appear to the group. I started with a brief "offering" gesture with my hands to say "I'm hoping to give you something". Next to me was a slim girl with neat short hair, scrubbed small face and wearing a skirt (the only one not in jeans). "I'm Joan", she said with a deep frown, a shake of her head and a flutter of her hands. We went back to this later when we'd gone round twice and I described how she'd appeared. She didn't know that she'd shaken her head. "But I always frown if I'm serious. I take this seriously". "Is that how you take yourself?" I asked and she nodded. John said his name very loudly, squaring his shoulders, and looking strong and happy. Much later when someone confessed they were a bit afraid of his great height and size, he replied that he didn't want to impress people with his strength. We reminded him of the forceful way in which he'd introduced himself. "Yes, well, perhaps I do a bit", he said sheepishly.

Barbara put her hands firmly on the floor in front of her as she said her name. "That was to show I have something to put into the group", she explained. I commented that it also looked as if she was seeking a firm base and she said, "Yes, that too". "I'm Cherry" was accompanied by a wide grin and an open-armed movement, very relaxed. Then we came to Andy, very quiet, nothing but the name, no "I am", no gesture, giving an impression that we could take him as and where he was or leave him — but for all that, he was still warm and secure. When I told him that this was how I perceived him he said yes, that was partly right but he felt shy. Then Dick spoke, stumbling over his name. What did that mean? Looking at me he said he was called Richard at home and Dick in college. I questioned him. Was Richard supposed to live up to parental expectations? He flushed, laughed and said it was true. "Think about who you are right now" I said. "I'm Dick", he said firmly.

We then split into pairs (I sat out) and did the "Tell me who you are?" exercise. Afterwards we discussed how frequently we describe ourselves by what we do (and judge others by what they do) and how difficult it is to get near to the core of our existence. The group also commented on the number of different selves we present to different people; and we linked this to their counselling work. Dick talked about social behaviour and taboos, physical contact. "Hey, yeah, when I was young", said Andy, "I used to be really embarrassed because I was short and thin. Suddenly I noticed that I'm not short and I've begun to enjoy my body; I mean, you know, just feel good about using my body". I suggested we explore this feeling and we walked around touching each other's hair, faces, hands, arms tentatively. There were some half-embarrassed hugs, lots of bursts of laughter and then somehow we were all in a close bunch holding each other, at first tightly, full of need and then peacefully and relaxed. We took it in turns to go into the middle of the circle, and let ourselves be gently rocked around inside it, with eyes closed. Before we finished the evening we shared feelings of trust and discussed whether we felt better being supported or giving support. "It's funny", Cherry said, "Sometimes it's hard to do one and sometimes it's hard to do the other". She paused. "But both can be beautiful can't they?"

The next morning I had an appointment to visit Mrs. J. Her twelve-year-old daughter had previously been referred to my agency for "persistent non-attendance and nervousness". Mrs. J. is about thirty, divorced, and also has a six-year-old son. When I began to look at the girl's problems I soon became aware that the mother was a highly neurotic young woman who had received quite a lot of psychiatric treatment in the previous years, and was convinced that she had a severe physical disability. It was obvious that the daughter was the presenting symptom for the mother's pain. Getting Karen back to school didn't prove too difficult. She wanted to write to her father but her mother kept making excuses about not knowing his address. After some discussion with Mrs. J. about her fears of Karen writing to her ex-husband, we did some straightforward bargaining. Karen would go back to school and Mum would contact the solicitor who had Dad's address.

Mrs. J. agreed to see me for six sessions to work on her own problems. She recounted a daunting list of real and imaginary ailments ranging from breast cancer (imagined), to hiatus hernia and peptic ulcer (ditto) to headaches, sore throats and earaches (real).By the time she saw me she had persuaded doctors to carry out innumerable tests on her, all of which proved negative. In fact, she had come up with a new complaint just before I came into her life. She was convinced that there was something wrong in her head. She had pains at the back, pains at the front, dizzy sensations, a weird jerky movement which she couldn't control and, worst of all, her brain was somehow becoming detached from her skull. She thought that it would soon begin to rattle around and eventually kill her! Her G.P. was utterly fed up with her and I began to think that if anything was rattling around inside Mrs. J. it was more likely to be the vast quantities of tablets he was prescribing (perhaps in self-defence?). The psychiatrist at the hospital after an incredulous gasp of "Oh! you mean you're actually treating her?" gave me his blessing to go ahead with obvious relief.

Monday was my third session with her. I had, until then, explored some of her family history with her and uncovered a desperately bad relationship with her father who had strongly rejected her. Indeed, the only nice thing she recalled about him was his long visit to her in the psychiatric hospital. So, I thought, perhaps she has to be sick or mad to get his care and attention. She also told me about her adolescent promiscuity and an abortion, and her feelings of guilt left over from this period. She skilfully opened up these and other tempting channels for me in those first sessions, only to leave me floundering in the mire each time I thought we were making progress. Last Monday I decided to go my way, not hers.

When she came in she was pale and miserable. Her head was worse, she was sure she had a tumour. She was sitting on a cushion on the floor and I sat on the floor too. Pulling a cushion off the settee I placed it firmly in front of her, a short distance from her, and explained what I wanted her to do. She was to imagine that her head was over on the cushion and she could talk to it. What would she want to say? Mrs. J. felt silly and awkward at first but soon relaxed enough to try. "Stop hurting, head!" She looked at me for encouragement, then said in a whining voice. "You give me an awful pain, if only you would stop hurting I would get better" (deep sigh). Then she said angrily *"Why* do you keep hurting?" "Is it hurting now?" I asked. "Yes, yes, all the time", she replied. I asked her to go and sit on the other cushion and imagine that she was her head talking to Jan (herself). She did as I suggested and immediately her face looked screwed-up and pained. I suggested she shut her eyes and described her existence as Jan's head. She looked tense, with tight shoulders, neck and face. A long pause. "I am all dark inside", she began, slowly. (She started to say "It is" instead of "I am" and I asked her to stick to "I" where possible). "I am full of pain and everything's sort of ... confused. I'm confused. My pain is at the back ... here ... no, it's all over ... here ... and here". She cradled her head in her arms and I said "What does Head say to Jan?" She gazed at the empty "Jan cushion" and said "Why don't you do something to make me better — I'm *your* head you know!" At this point I told her to go back to the other cushion and be Jan again. "Answer your head" I said.

She looked thoughtfully at the fantasy head, frowned and

suddenly said to me, "It's me isn't it? I mean, my head's telling me to do something about it". "And can you?" I asked. She shrugged. "I don't know". "Where's your pain now?" I asked, "It's gone" she replied. "Oh really? What made it go?" She laughed and said "I suppose I did". I ended the session after a few more quiet minutes without offering any interpretations of my own. Just as I was leaving she made two remarks. First she said "You're not an ordinary social worker are you?" in a very suspicious tone. I laughed and said I was — but I sometimes did extraordinary things. Then she said, "But what if I panic before next week?" I said that she would probably survive her panic and she could tell me about it next week! Mrs. J.'s head pains and delusions disappeared and I don't think they will come back. She's developed a chest pain instead and I am not sure where I will go from here. I somehow can't see us laying her whole anatomy bit by bit, in fantasy, onto a cushion!

On Tuesday something happened which reminded me vividly how valuable it is to play with children and to be alert to the message they give you by their actions. I am always fascinated by the non-verbal level of communication and with children this can be especially rich. Ian had been attending clinic for a couple of years before my first contact with him and his family. He is twelve-years-old, very withdrawn, sufferes from asthma and a stammer and is a chronic encopretic (soiler). At first he wouldn't see me without his mother but now he chooses to see me alone. We don't talk much and I am learning that he tells me what he needs to through his playing. A session spent in the sandpit (we are lucky to have a well-equipped playroom) getting rather mucky means that he soiled a lot the week before; a game of "boxes" on the blackboard with Ian drawing lots of tiny, tight, rigid squares means he feels boxed in. Last week his mother told me that the sudden marked improvement in his asthma and soiling had relapsed and he'd had a bad week. I went with him into the playroom and after a few moments he chose to play with a set of chunky wooden blocks of different shapes and sizes. He soon started to build. Walls, paths ... after half an hour during which he would barely answer any remarks or questions, he stopped and we looked at his work. The front was an intricate facade, constructed with care and imagination. Archways, windows, entrances and exits. Immediately behind the facade, however, instead of the expected rooms of a "castle" he had put a solid blockade of bricks, totally impenetrable, unassailable. At the rear of this mass was an exit ("a back passage" was the phrase which came into my mind!).

After a while I said to Ian, "Show me where *you* are today", and he went to the back, placing his building between us. "Well, I can't reach you there", I said and we smiled at each other without any challenge. We were sitting on the floor and I lay down on my side of the fortress so that my face was now almost at floor level and said, "If I come right down to where your building is, I can't see you at all". After a few minutes he came around the blocks on his hands and knees, and sat with me at the front. He said slowly, "My father doesn't talk to me. He only likes Sally" (his little sister). For the rest of the session which was scheduled for an hour, he talked more freely than ever before and went away with an unusual smile and lack of tension. Incidentally, I had failed to engage Ian's father in family therapy — he wouldn't talk to me either!

The importance of picking up the clues given by one's clients is often demonstrated by children. Sarah (aged seven) was a lovely example some time ago. I had previously interviewed her mother and had got a detailed history and background from her. Mother and father were divorced and the mother now lived with a cohabitee together with Sarah and her two other children. The presenting problem, referred by the mother herself, was Sarah's tantrums in school and at home and her general defiant and naughty manner in the family. Then I saw Sarah for the first time. When I entered the waiting room I found the child in tears and mother looking cross and embarrassed. I sat down beside Sarah and introduced myself, talking to her, arousing her interest long enough to stem the tears. I pointed to the pictures of baby animals on the wall and she smiled at the kitten, the puppy, the foal. When we came to a little fox, she shuddered violently and shook her head, but I attached no special significance to that. After that she was willing to come with me to the play room.

I asked her if she knew why she had come. (It's not unusual for children to think they coming to see the dentist!) Sarah said immediately and very positively, "Because I have bad dreams". I was surprised — during my earlier meeting with her mother I had been told that she slept well and was not troubled by dreams. However, if that was where Sarah wanted to start, it was fine with me and I asked her to tell me about one of her dreams. Whilest we talked we wandered around, examining the toys (I felt she would be too restricted by sitting down opposite me) and she started to tell me about a dream where she was chased by a fox. I hadn't given her the chance to tell me in the waiting room, so she'd made another opportunity. The story was not of primary importance but the imagery was. In her dream she was chased, frightened, lost, helpless, and could not find a safe place in unfamiliar surroundings. She stopped near the blackboard which covers one wall of the room and I gave her the box of coloured chalks and asked her to draw her dream. Eagerly, and in great detail, she drew first a truly fearsome-looking fox and then another. At last she stepped back, looked at her picture and shuddered. Catching hold of my hand she asked if I was frightened. I told her I was a little bit and she whispered, "So am I".

I said to her, "Say something to your foxes — what do you want to say?" Still whispering she replied, "Go away". I encouraged her to try saying it louder and louder until she was shouting the phrase at the top of her voice, her gaze fixed on the blackboard. Suddenly she wrote on the board "GO AWAY FOXS". "Can you make them?" I asked. She picked up the duster and, using every scrap of her energy, she rubbed and rubbed till the board was clean. Completely absorbed and out of breath from the effort, she then wrote in chalk "THEY HAV GON". In the twelve weeks I saw her she never had another really frightening dream. She often used dreams as a way of sharing anxieties, but she became more cooperative at home and her mother's complaints about her turned into praise.

I suppose, for many of us, our choice of work and the methods we use reflect some inner need of our own. I need people. I frequently need to be alone so that I can enjoy my own space and experience myself and my existence within it but more often I need to explore the quality of the space which links me to and separates me from other people. That is why I find that working with families and groups is so exciting and rewarding. I also talk too much. I can talk myself into — and out of — anything. That is why I learned the value of non-verbal methods of communicating and why I use non-verbal signals so much in my work. This sometimes means looking for non-verbal clues and making people aware of them and sometimes it means deliberately setting up a structure in which people have to communicate without words. Here are some examples.

Martin, seventeen years old, had committed offences for which he was on probation. An ex-drug addict, with a history of non-attendance at school and delinquent behaviour, he and his parents were engaged in family therapy. At each session Martin firmly seated himself between his parents. At the third session I asked him, "Is that where you like to be — between Mum and Dad?" He shrugged as if to dismiss the question and then said, "No. That's where they like me to be". I invited him to change place and we ended up with the parents next to each other. What followed was long and complex but, released from his focal position of "piggy-in-the-middle" Martin was able to face his parents as a separate individual and his behaviour began to mature and stabilize. Parents now found they had to talk directly to each other rather than via Martin. Their covert grievances became overt and therefore available for therapy. Simply by sticking to his seating plan until I had got the message, Martin achieved his goal of bringing his family's problem into the open.

In another family, Mrs. G. sat throughout an initial family meeting clutching a diary which she had removed from her handbag. She kept it half-hidden and glanced surreptitiously at it from time to time. Somehow, I managed not to see this during the session — each time I began to focus on it, another member of the family would engage my attention. However, Mrs. G. was determined and she repeated this action at the next meeting. This time I said to her, "It look as though you've got a secret that you're not sure about sharing". "Oh no!" she said sharply putting the diary back in her handbag. I kept my attention on her and suddenly she blurted out "Debra's adopted you know — we've never talked about it though". There it was, the dark family secret which she'd been both yearning and afraid to tell.

Family sculpting is a good example of a contrived method of inducing non-verbal communication — this is a whole subject on its own. I only have space to give one example here.

Paul and Stella were fifteen-year-old twins with a brother, Tim, who was eight years old. Both parents worked. Paul was on probation and his probation officer and I were working as co-therapists with the family. There were interminable family quarrels over every aspect of their life and the recurring theme was the twins' lack of cooperation with household chores. Work rotas didn't help and the mother continued to nag them that they had no family feeling, no idea of sharing, no consideration for each other. Paul, the least verbally articulate, was labelled a trouble-maker and I decided to use him to sculpt his family. I explained that I wanted him to arrange his family in a way that would express how he saw the way things were. With my guidance, going slowly, he first placed his father and Tim on the settee together looking at a toy, close and self-contained. Then he put Stella a little way from them, on the floor watching T.V. He then placed his mother in a far corner, with her back to them all "doing the ironing". Finally he put himself at the far end of the settee. Even before I had a chance to ask them how their positions felt, Mother said, "This feels awful! Why am I so cut off? I don't like it!". Paul said to me, "As soon as she comes in she makes us move. We can only be together when she's out". Mother began to cry. Father said gently, "It's true, love. As soon as you come in from work you're on to us all to do this, do that. You're never at peace with us". I asked them to show me what happened.

Mother walked to the middle of the room and immediately everyone got up and scattered, looking cross and miserable. They then returned to their first position. I asked Paul where he would like his mother to be. "Here, with us", he said. She shook her head. "There's no room for me". "Try it", I said. "Oh, they're fine as they are without me", she replied with a long suffering sigh. I challenged her. "Oh! so you really like it out there?" With an effort she moved in and sat on the floor near the settee. Stella came nearer and they all sat and looked at each other, smiling. "This feels lovely", said Paul and they all nodded. Then mother said, "It's funny. I never realized I was pulling them apart".

Sculpting, like any other contrived device sounds phony, and gimmicky until you experience it. Used skilfully it is a powerful, constructive, and meaningful way of helping people to gain insight into their relationships — and to change them. I use methods which feel comfortable and good for me. I set tasks, so that a family has a positive link with the therapist, a stepping-stone from one session to the next and a shared achievement (be it success or failure) to bring with them. Sometimes these tasks are paradoxical (intended to make the client do the opposite).

Susan was a difficult sulky fifteen-year-old who lived with her mother. They hardly spoke a civil word to each other and mother complained that Susan never confided in her. "We just can't communicate", she said. "I don't want to confide in her!" snapped Susan. "Quite right", I said. "What you two are really good at is keeping your secrets to yourselves. Only you're not doing it quite well enough". I went on to instruct them that for the next two weeks Susan must not tell her mother anything about her thoughts, feelings, or activities. On no account was she to confide anything of importance. I told Mrs. W. to continue asking Susan lots of questions about where she'd been, and who she was with. "Well, that's the way it is anyway" they both muttered angrily. After one week Mrs. W. phoned on an obvious pretext of having forgotten the appointment time. Then she said apologetically, "I'm afraid we haven't been very good at doing what you said. After all Susan does have a right to some privacy". I chided her gently and told her to try harder. They arrived for their next meeting with shame-faced grins. "We tried but we couldn't do it". "But you've been doing it for ages!" I exclaimed. Apparently, once Mrs. W. had gone against my instruction (that is she had stopped nagging her daughter), Susan had happily begun to confide in her and their relationship improved enormously. "After all", Susan said, "She is my mother and I ought to be able to tell her things".

Now and again I do something phony and don't realize until too late. A few months ago a ten-year-old boy said to me, "You're bleedin' daft you are. You get on my nerves always wanting to know what we feel about fings".

Well, you can't win 'em all.

Creative Social Work

SUGGESTIONS FOR FURTHER READING

Roy Bailey and Mike Brake (eds), *Radical Social Work,* Arnold, 1975.

John Berger, *A Fortunate Man,* Penguin, 1967.

Juliet Berry, *Daily Experience in Residential Life,* Routledge and Kegan Paul, 1975.

Arthur Blumberg and Robert Golembieski, *Learning and Change in Groups,* Penguin, 1976.

Jimmy Boyle, *A Sense of Freedom,* Pan, 1977.

David Brandon, *Zen in the Art of Helping,* Routledge and Kegan Paul, 1976.

Hannah Green, *I Never Promised You a Rose Garden,* Pan, 1964.

Tom Hart, *Safe on a See-Saw,* Quartet Books, 1977.

Bruce Hugman, *Act Natural,* Bedford Square Press, 1977.

Bill Jordan, *Helping in Social Work,* Routledge and Kegan Paul, 1979.

Carl Jung (ed.), *Man and his Symbols,* Picador, 1978.

Barbara Kahan, *Growing Up in Care,* Blackwell, 1979.

Alan Keith-Lucas, *Giving and Taking Help,* University of North Carolina Press, 1972.

Ken Kesey, *One Flew Over the Cuckoo's Nest,* Picador, 1962.

George Konrad, *The Caseworker,* Hutchinson, 1975.

Krishnamurti, *Beginnings of Learning,* Pelican, 1978.

John C. Lilly, *The Centre of the Cyclone,* Paladin, 1973.

Groucho Marx, *The Groucho Letters,* Sphere Books, 1976.

Thomas Merton, *The Way of Chuang Tzu,* Unwin, 1965.

George Orwell, *The Road to Wigan Pier,* Penguin, 1937.

Geoffrey Pearson, *The Deviant Imagination,* Macmillan, 1975.

Robert Pirsig, *Zen and the Art of Motorcycle Maintenance,* The Bodley Head, 1974.

Laurens Van Der Post, *A Story Like the Wind,* Penguin, 1974.

Mike Simpkins, *Trapped Within Welfare,* Macmillan, 1979.

Jane Sparrow, *Diary of a Student Social Worker,* Routledge and Kegan Paul, 1978.

Jane Sparrow, *Diary of a Delinquent Episode,* Routledge and Kegan Paul, 1977.

Daphne Statham, *Radicals in Social Work,* Routledge and Kegan Paul, 1978.

Anthony Storr, *The Dynamics of Creation,* Pelican, 1976.

Chogyam Trungpa, *Meditation in Action,* Stuart and Watkins, 1969.

INDEX

Index

134